EDUCATION, ECOLOGY AND DEVELOPMENT

EDUCATION, ECOLOGY AND DEVELOPMENT

The Case for an Education Network

Edited by

Colin Lacey and Roy Williams

WWF

KOGAN PAGE

Co-published in 1987 by
The World Wildlife Fund
and
Kogan Page Ltd, 120 Pentonville Road, London N1 9JN

British Library Cataloguing in Publication Data

Lacey, Colin
    Education, ecology and development : the
    case for an education network.
    1. Environmental education
    I. Title   II. Williams, Roy
    333.7′07   GF26

    ISBN 1-85091-495-8

Photoset in North Wales by
Derek Doyle & Associates, Mold, Clwyd.
Printed and bound in Great Britain at
The Camelot Press Ltd. Southampton

CONTENTS

CONTRIBUTORS

John Abraham is Tutor of Food and Society at the University of Sussex. His interests include research in food and development and development of curriculum materials on food policy. He previously researched in areas such as food additive control and the social processes of schooling. He is co-author of *The Penguin Dictionary of Food Additives*.

Andy Hargreaves recently lectured at the University of Warwick and is now Associate Professor in Education at the Ontario Institute for Studies in Education, Toronto, Canada. He is the author of *Two Cultures of Schooling*, (Falmer Press, 1986) and has edited a number of other books on curriculum and classroom issues including *Curriculum Practice: some sociological casestudies* (Falmer Press, 1983) (with Martyn Hammersley) and *Classroom and Staffrooms: the sociology of teachers and teaching* (Open University Press, 1984) (with Peter Woods).

John Huckle teaches geography at Bedford College of Higher Education. He edited *Geographical Education: reflection and action* (Open University Press, 1983) and has written many articles on geographical and environmental education. A member of World Wildlife UK's education advisory panel, he is also on the editorial panel of *Contemporary Issues in Geography and Education* and a member of the Socialist Environment and Resources Association. During 1987–88, he will be seconded to WWF-UK to finish writing up the project described in this book. (Readers can contact him at Bedford College of Higher Education on 0235 51671.)

Professor Colin Lacey started his teaching career as a science teacher in a London Comprehensive school. After returning to Manchester University to read for a PhD in Sociology he has specialized in research into education. He now teaches at the University of Sussex. His publications include *Hightown Grammar* and *The Socialisation of Teachers*. His interest in ecology and development stem from his political interest in world systems and visits to Third World countries.

David Pepper is Principal Lecturer in Geography at Oxford Polytechnic. He teaches courses on environmentalism, and war and peace studies. He is author of *The Roots of Modern Environmentalism* (Croom Helm, 1986) and co-editor of *The Geography of Peace and War* (Blackwell, 1985) and *Nuclear Power in Crisis* (Croom Helm/Nicholson, 1987). He has written papers on environmental politics, geography and defence strategies and geographical education. His current research is on alternative communities and environmental futures.

Geoff Whitty is Head of the Department of Education at Bristol Polytechnic. His interest in ecology, development and education is part of a broad interest in curriculum development, especially in the field of issue-based humanities courses. He is co-author (with D Gleeson) of *Development in Social Studies Teaching* (Open Books, 1976) and *Sociology and School Knowledge* (Methuen, 1985).

Roy Williams is a Research Fellow in the School of Education, University of Sussex, working mainly in the field of environmental and development education. He has been involved with several curriculum projects including: the global environmental education programme for the World Wildlife Fund, United Nation's Children's Fund's *Children and World Development* (Richmond Publishing Company Ltd, Summer 1987) and is presently conducting a research project on teacher education and the global environment.

INTRODUCTION

Colin Lacey,
University of Sussex

The papers presented in this book were written as a result of a conference called at the University of Sussex by two researchers and educators who had become puzzled, or perhaps more accurately deeply concerned, by the total lack of recognition given to two important contradictions facing the future of humankind. They can be stated very simply but they are very complex issues involving the interplay of vast physical, ecological, economic and social systems.

Development and Developing Countries

The first contradiction concerns the notions of 'development' and 'developing countries'. It is a well established belief that developing countries which are well managed and politically stable will, over a period of time, join the developed countries in a high standard of living that could eventually extend to all the countries of the world. Indeed the belief is central to the whole idea of development and the concept of a 'developing country'. A good example of the shared nature of this belief was illustrated recently in a television programme where Princess Anne was being questioned by Scottish schoolchildren. One girl asked the Princess if she did not feel ashamed or uncomfortable sometimes when, as President of the Save the Children Fund, she walked among poor or starving children. The girl asking the question was referring to the great discrepancy of wealth between the rich princess and the poverty stricken children. The princess replied that no, she did not feel worried or embarrassed by this problem. The solution to the problems faced by these children did not rest in giving away our wealth but by going among them and teaching them the things that we know so that they could help themselves and attain our standards of health, education and civilization. The audience applauded and the questioning moved on.

1

Gross National Product

There is, of course, an important truth in this answer – it is more useful to teach people to help themselves – but there is also an important untruth. At the centre of our wealth and standards of health and education lies an economic system based on a complex and advanced industrial technology and controlled by a system of finance and ownership called capitalism. Generally speaking, the greater the accumulation of capital in a country, the more advanced and productive the industry of that country is likely to be and the higher the standards of life (education and health). Wealthy countries, therefore, also consume far more of the world's resources and raw materials to sustain and develop their standard of life. This productivity based on the manufacturing and service industries of a country is roughly measured by a device used by economists, the gross national product (GNP). It is instructive to look at the way GNP is distributed among the countries of the world, if we are interested in the possibility of the poor achieving the levels of productivity or consumption of the rich.

Table 1 *Gross National Product per Head of Population for Four Categories of Nation (1982)*

Number of Countries in each Income Category		Range of GNP per Head of Population in Dollars	Population in each Category
Low Income Economies	34	80 – 390	2,266 million
Middle Income Economies	38	440 – 1,610	1,158 million
Upper Middle Income Economies	22	1,680 – 6,840	489 million
Industrial Market Economies	19	5,150 – 17,010	723 million

NOTE: *The table excludes Eastern European non market economies (8) and High Income oil exporters (5)*

Source: *World Development Report 1984*

The message is startling. It shows that only a small proportion of the world's population shares in the modern consumer society with high levels of health and education. It also suggests that only a small number can ever participate in this way of life. The table contains two major distortions that we must explain before proceeding.

The first distortion is that the concept of GNP does not extend to all goods and services produced in a country. If a farmer grows a crop for his own consumption or barters the crop for other goods and

Figure 1   *Range of GNP against Population*

Pop. in
100 mills

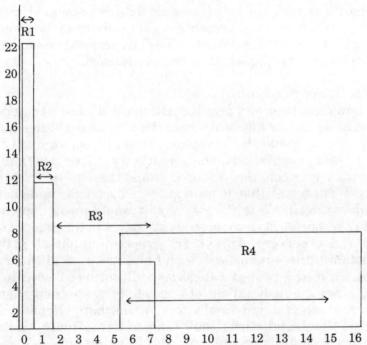

GNP per annum per head of population in thousands of dollars

R1 = range of GNP for low category countries, eg Kenya, Pakistan, Bangladesh, Chad.
R2 = range of GNP for middle category countries, eg Colombia, Turkey, Senegal, Sudan.
R3 = range of GNP for upper middle category countries, eg Singapore, Hong Kong, Malaysia, Syria.
R4 = range of GNP for industrial market countries, eg Switzerland, Sweden, USA, Spain, Ireland.

services this is not recorded. The table therefore exaggerates the poverty of the poorest nations with respect to goods and services produced and consumed in the traditional sector. However, it does represent people's share of the modern economy so it does reflect their share of motor cars, televisions, medicines, modern fuels, fashionable clothes, books and other items which characterize modern living. It follows that if the poorer countries were ever in a position to demand their share of these things there would either have to be a massive redistribution of them on a world scale or a rapid depletion of the world's resources leading to an ecological crisis.

The second distortion lies in the way the table is presented. In order to simplify a mass of statistics the table presents four categories of nation. The range of GNP represented by the four categories is very wide. If the same data is presented in a block diagram (Figure 1) it presents a more accurate picture of the dimensions recorded in the data. The diagram also gives examples of countries at the top and bottom of each category.

The power of the wealthy

It is now clear how very poor the nations in the lowest category are and how wide the range is between the nations in the most wealthy categories. It should also be apparent that with such a small number of the world's population in the top category (16 per cent) and such a large gap between the resources consumed by the richest and poorest categories that if poorest were ever able to demand the standards available to the wealthy, it would mean depleting the world's resources of raw materials by factors in the order of tens (or thousands of per cent). This kind of prospect is untenable in the near or distant future on an earth with finite resources. It follows that countries in the poorest categories will not be allowed to do so. Should any group of nations organize to increase their share then they can expect rapid retaliation rather than sympathy. These attempts (and retaliations) could take the form of market manipulation, trade controls or rights over land or resources. The West's response to OPEC was an example of using trade controls and the Falklands conflict an example of using rights over land.

The power of the richest nations in protecting their advantages is exercised in many complex and often hidden ways. It rests in the control of large amounts of capital, in the domination of markets and their ability to control the terms of trade between the richer and poorer sectors of the market: sometimes it rests on their control of armed force and sophisticated weaponry. A further important power factor is the ideology of public discussion. It remains the case that most wealthy populations believe that their wealth is fully justified by a fair system of exchange and that where poverty exists it is largely the fault of the poor. The concept of 'developing country' is an important concept within this dominant ideology within the powerful rich nations. It implies that things are improving and despite present day poverty, famines and natural catastrophies, the world is becoming a better place. We should, therefore, examine the trends as they affect the rich and poor nations.

The trends, in terms of differentiation, at the present time are not encouraging. The rich countries of the world maintain or increase their share of wealth while the poor make little progress and in many cases sink further behind in the unequal race for resources. The average rate of growth of economies in the low income category (in Table 1) between 1960 and 1982 was 3 per cent. However, this group includes China with a massive population of over one billion and a growth rate of 5 per cent. If China is excluded, as it should be because it is not a free market economy subject to the kind of market forces we have been describing, then the average growth rates for this group is about 1.2 per cent. It should be noted that eight countries in this group had negative growth rates over this period of 22 years. In contrast the industrial market economies had an average annual growth rate of 3.3 per cent.

In absolute terms this difference is very large. 3.3 per cent of the mid-point of the range for industrial economies is $366 while 1.3 per cent of the mid-point for low income countries is $3. This represents the average amount that would be added to each person's income in the next year if growth rates remained stable. This is clearly not a recipe for greater equality. Nor does it encourage the belief that the so-called 'developing countries' have been doing much 'developing'.

The trends described above are long-term and have been discernible since the earliest records have been available. In the short-term, particularly over the last four or five years, things seem to have become a lot worse. A recent paragraph in *The State of the World's Children 1987* describes the worsening situation:

> 'Stagnating trade, falling commodity prices, declining aid, mounting debt repayments and a steep drop in private lending, have stalled economic development in many countries during this decade. Between 1980 and 1985, average incomes fell in 17 out of 23 countries in Latin America and in 24 out of 32 countries in sub-Saharan Africa. Overall, average incomes fell by 9 per cent in Latin America and by 15 per cent in Africa.'

In the countries where these falls have occurred the concrete result has been declining health and education services and deteriorating health and nutrition. It is normal in our world today that 14 million young children die every year and that millions more live incomplete lives damaged by malnutrition and ill-health. Most of these deaths and most cases of ill-health are preventable. The reasons for the continuation and indeed increase are not lack of scientific or technical knowledge. They are political and social reasons and they reside in an economic system and its sustaining ideologies which renders the weak weaker and blames poverty on the poor while the rich continue to accumulate wealth and power.

The 'contradiction in development' can now be clearly stated. The rich countries of the world hold out an example of progress and material comfort to the poor countries. They encourage them to participate in a process of development that promises to bring them all up to living standards comparable with the rich. Yet that promise is unrealizable for ecological and economic reasons. In fact we shall see that the more the poor struggle to produce more products to sell to the rich the less likely they are to enrich themselves.

There are a number of methods of comparing the world prices of primary products and manufactured goods. The World Bank uses the manufactured unit value (MUV) index as a deflator because it reflects changes in the prices at which developing countries can buy or sell on the world market. According to The World Development Report,

> 'the price trend for 33 non-fuel commodities ... has been one of sharp decline. Using the MUV deflator, the combined price index of these commodities stood at 160 in 1970, at 100 in 1977–9 and at 84 in 1984. This represents a halving of the purchasing power of raw materials in terms of manufactured goods.'

They are caught in a trap in which they compete among each other and impoverish themselves as the goods they produce become cheaper and undercut the market. The poor can only be helped if the rich change the way in which they live and trade. Yet the rich control the debate about poverty and maintain that the fate of the poor rests in their own hands saying that they must work harder to produce more – a 'Catch 22' situation.

A final illustration of this complex set of forces can be seen in the case of the most developed and powerful nation. The United States of America represents 7 per cent of the world's population yet it consumes 35 per cent of the world's resources. No other country can expect to attain this pre-eminence and, as we have seen, the possibility of the great majority of other countries ever achieving these levels of affluence is almost unthinkable. Yet if we look at the problems of poverty in the USA they remain unsolved. On many of the indicators of poverty the poor within the USA show the results of deprivation and neglect to a greater extent than others in less wealthy countries. In other words, it is not just the creation of wealth that solves poverty – if this were the case the USA would have removed poverty by now. The problem of poverty resides within the way that wealth is created, by whom and for whom, and the way the rich and the powerful organize the distribution of the wealth created. The poor are very rarely in a position to determine these things.

It follows that if we are ever to solve the problem of poverty on a world scale then the rich countries must quite radically change their present behaviour. But what hope is there of this when for centuries the rich have exploited the poor and invented very good reasons why it is both just and necessary to do so? If we look at history then the record of moral argument, whether it be religious or secular, reformist or revolutionary, has not been very encouraging. On the question of world poverty we already have a large number of books, reports, governmental statements and even international agencies which put the case for change, yet little happens unless poverty develops into famine and crisis.

The 'Failure of Success'

We hope that this situation will change. The reason for hoping this lies in the second contradiction that concerned us in calling the conference. We can call this contradiction the 'failure of success'. Once more it simplifies complex ecological, economic and social systems and relates one to another to provide a model or framework for analysis. The explanation of this contradiction begins with an understanding of the extraordinary success of the capitalist system.

Even in its earliest period capitalism proved to be a remarkable 'revolutionary' combination of financial and technological innovations that could remake social and economic relationships very rapidly and cause substantial social change. It did this by rearranging the factors of production, by putting them in the hands of a new class of people, the bourgeoisie, but also by making available goods and services at such low prices that in the 20th Century the ordinary person living in a developed capitalist country is able to enjoy a standard of life in many ways superior to that of the wealthiest aristocrats of two or three hundred years ago.

Printing

A good illustration of this progress is the development of printing. The invention of printing was not a European innovation. It had been developed in an advanced form by the Chinese to print paper banknotes many years before. In addition, the Koreans had developed a method for the mass production of library texts. Neither innovation developed in such a way as to produce the kinds of effects experienced within capitalism. The unique quality of the European re-invention of printing in the 15th Century was the fact that by this time all the main ingredients of the capitalist system were then in place and the innovation could produce the astounding growth and rapid social change that we have come to take for granted. J Burke (1985) describes printing as the answer to a problem. Economic development had proceeded rapidly after the black death but commercial progress was limited by the lack of scribes and the very high price of copyists.

Within 30 years of the development in Gutenburg of the first hand operated printing press using metal type, printing had spread to every major European city. The price of a new book in Florence fell to less than 1/300th of its pre-printing cost. Burke describes the print shop as the first truly capitalist venture with the printer

'responsible for finding investors, organizing supplies and labour, setting up production schedules, coping with strikes, having highly qualified assistance and analysing the market for printed texts. He was also in intense competition with other printers ...'

The obvious outcome of the cheapening of printing was the increase in sales of books. The wider distribution of existing texts, for example the bible, was the most obvious immediate outcome but this was quickly followed by books on how to practise the many crafts and skills that were developing at a great pace. Accurate knowledge was disseminated on a large scale.

Printing disseminated both information and misinformation with equal facility. The widespread distribution (and sale) of printed indulgences or pardons to increase the power and wealth of the Vatican was one development that led Martin Luther to produce his 92 criticisms of the church. Printing inevitably became a major factor in the ideological war that followed and within three years of Luther's first act of rebellion 300,000 copies of his work had been sold. The broadsheet became a feature of all future political and religious dispute. It stimulated the demand for education and led to great struggles about what could and could not be printed or read. The multiple ramifications of this development are too numerous to trace. We need to note only three.

1. Technical innovation in the hands of capitalist owners has continued to expand and reshape the printing industry with vast forests being cut every year to supply an ever expanding industry based on fewer workers.
2. The capitalist class has gained in power until it controls all the major productive forces and all the major institutions of society including the state.
3. This effort by individual capitalists shapes and expands consumer demand so that our society is now being changed and developed at an amazing pace by successful capitalists.

Industrial high technology

If the marriage between capitalism and industrial technology and now high technology produces such dynamism and such rapid progress as printing why should we be cautious about the present day effects of this union and anxious for the future? The answer to this question explains our second contradiction — the 'failure of success'. At the beginning of the industrial revolution humankind was still dwarfed by the forces of nature. It was possible to see the natural resources of the world as unlimited and capable of recovering from even the most heavy onslaughts that human beings could muster. Today this imbalance of power is reversed. Humankind has the power to plunder from almost any environment and to destroy the very foundations of our life: the soil, the seas, lakes and rivers, the forests and natural habitats of countless species and even the atmosphere. Despite the fact that we now have advanced and accurate knowledge of this destruction, we are powerless to act on the information because we lack initiatives that are predicated on collective interests and collective responsibility. Instead our major institutions are founded on capitalist imperatives that recognize only the major constraints and opportunities of the capitalist system, in particular the profit imperative. In this system there are no brakes, and very few means of slowing down destruction. It will continue to expand on the basis of profitable exploitation until the resource has disappeared or the environment has been destroyed.

A startling example of this kind of destruction is being acted out within the tropical rainforests, particularly in the largest and most important complex of forests in Brazil. These enormous and geologically stable ecosystems have probably been evolving since the Cretaceous period; for about 60 million years. They contain about half the world's species. The Amazon basin alone contains about one sixth of the world's fresh water. It has a major influence on climatic patterns including the wind pattern that generates and sustains the Gulf Stream, which in turn makes the British Isles and the Nordic countries habitable on the present scale. Despite its tremendous importance in terms of present-day climatic stability, its future importance as a genetic store house and its importance to the present population of Indians and rubber tappers, it is being destroyed. At the present rate it will be cleared in the next two to three decades; already in the last ten years an area the size of Europe has been cleared. The reason for its destruction resides in its present-day profitability to international capitalists, the Brazilian government and Brazilian capitalists. In the short run it is possible to use it as a source of timber (pulp and tropical hardwood) and minerals; as a source of new rough pasture for beef cattle; and as a place for resettling peasant farmers displaced from warm temperate farmlands by plantation agriculture. The Brazilian government pursues this policy as a way of earning foreign exchange to pay off its debt to international bankers, and as a way of defusing political pressure from displaced peasant farmers. Both of these policy needs result from pressures from international finance, in particular, the increase in interest rates and the drop of international commodity prices. The working of the capitalist system is therefore intimately intertwined with the destruction of the tropical rainforests.

Clearly, there are many who would dispute the scenario. It has been argued that advanced technology can solve the problem of shortages, especially the problem of energy. In addition, it is pointed out that many capitalist organizations have acted with responsibility towards the environment and set up rules to govern extraction and exploitation. This is an important case and we are certainly not advocating that it should be ignored. Our experience, however, is that it is theoretically flawed and that in practice it seldom succeeds in producing the required outcomes of a productive process in harmony with the natural environment. Instead resources are depleted, soils compacted or eroded, rivers and the atmosphere polluted on a scale that threatens the long-term existence of many environments essential to the well being of humankind. The examples of radio-active pollution from nuclear power stations, the destruction of the tropical rainforests, the damaging of the ozone layer and acid rain destruction of fish life and forests are only the most recent and spectacular examples of this process. These examples and many others cast a deep shadow over the spectacular success of the capitalist system as we know it. Its major features: the free and open competition of the market place; the freedom of individuals to pursue their own advantage, regardless of the outcome for others and the vast accumulation of capital in the hands of a few, must now be brought into question.

These features have of course been challenged before. Previous challenges have been on the basis of the moral outcomes of capitalism – marked inequality and hardship for the masses (Christian socialist and Fabian); or have been in terms of the structural contradictions within capitalism – its failure to address the problem of differentiation, alienation and class formation (Marx). The present challenge acknowledges the partial success of capitalism in solving some of these problems within the advanced capitalist nation states (although it would seem they have reappeared on an international scale). In addition, however, it brings into question the very basis of capitalist success – the enormous, uncontrollable dynamism of the system in creating 'wealth'. It is this process that will have to be controlled if the long-term disaster predicted here is to be avoided.

Consumerism

There is one final element in the argument that needs to be explained before the full force of the 'failure of success' contradiction can be understood. The capitalist system is not just based on efficient methods of manufacture and the twin harnessing of technological and financial systems: it has also been successful in supplying the goods and services that the consumer wants. One of the reasons capitalism is capable of destroying traditional systems is that it supplies goods and services which people prefer to those offered by traditional crafts and cultures. Capitalism, in its mature stage, is therefore a twin-engined machine, pushed by the search for profit but pulled by the desire for the goods it produces. The fine tuning of these two engines by capitalist governments and capitalist producer organizations has developed a culture in which there is a never-ending stream of products promising new experiences, new facilities, new powers, new freedoms and new designs for new tastes and fashions. Consumers are made to feel that there is always something new and worthwhile to reach for, whether it be a new sweat shirt, a new motor car, a new private plane, an automatic pilot or the fourth or fifth residence. There is no end to the process of demand and, therefore, no end to the process of striving for more. Most importantly, there is no provision for, or encouragement of, large numbers of individuals to feel that they are wealthy or rich enough or over provided for: there are always things that others have got, that they need or feel they should have. The people of the developing world or even the poor within the industrial world do not have a high priority in this situation of constantly unfulfilled demand.

The Education System

The tension of consumer demand within capitalist societies is no longer left to chance. The new information networks of newspaper, radio, cinema and television keep up a constant bombardment of information and sensation that exploits every impressionable aspect of the human species. It has effectively created a new total education system in which culture is shaped and consumption adjusted through advertisements and the penetration of the enter-tainment, sport and political worlds. It is at this point in its development that the system is most powerful but also most vulnerable. At the point where the consumer, that is the citizen, falls under the spell of the capitalist producer there is no longer a major independent force looking at the system from a critical or alternative perspective. This education system is without a pilot and if the interests of powerful capitalists will be met by destroying a precious resource then there are few mechanisms for stopping. Also there are increasingly fewer methods of educating the public or informing them on ways that will ensure that collective, long-term interests are safeguarded.

The Aims of the Book

The education system remains one of the few systems that retains some autonomy in the face of a coordinated attack to bring its aims and practices in line with the interests of capitalism. We aim to set up a debate which looks carefully at the relationship between capitalist social systems and the natural environment and the quality of life that is promised to future generations. We believe that it is now important that these questions are opened up for examination by all generations but particularly by students and pupils in our schools. It is they who will inherit the world that we are transforming in what appears to be a one-way process.

In exploring the destructive trends within capitalism we do not wish to imply that socialism would provide an automatic solution. In many cases socialist countries have shown a similar disregard of the environment. We are stressing these particular trends in capitalism because capitalism represents the dominant world system and these trends represent the present-day outcome of the system. Socialism plays a correspondingly minor role and is presently represented by very few varieties in the wide range of possibilities available. The highly centralized socialist systems of Eastern Europe are not regarded by writers in this volume either as 'typical socialism' or as the inevitable outcome of socialist policies. We are advocating a process of exploration and study which does not limit itself to existing forms of capitalism or socialism.

The process we are advocating is not a rigid indoctrination or a narrow focus on the politics of parties and interest groups. It is a broadening of the school curriculum and the public debate with respect to these issues so that the process of education in school and the debate out-of-school merges with and enhances the 'realness' of the issues. For example, we would agree with the idea proposed by Sir Keith Joseph and taken up by Kenneth Baker that pupils should study 'the wealth creating process' and that pupils should 'understand industry'. We ask that this understanding develop within the context of the whole world system of competing economies and the limitations of the material environment. We would want to point out that the long-term disaster that awaits us is as indifferent to socialist rhetoric as it is to capitalist ideology. Most socialist parties are almost as indifferent to the environment and just as attracted to growth as capitalist parties. The debate we hope to foster is likely to require an equally fundamental rethink for socialists as for any other major political grouping. I personally see more promise in the socialist response because the theoretical stance taken by socialists seems to promise a more open, democratic and, in the long term, more collectively intelligent response to the problems. This is not the place to discuss in detail the contrasting characteristics of socialism and capitalism (this issue is dealt with in greater detail in Lacey's paper) but short definitions could be of use to the reader in negotiating the papers in the book. Even dictionaries appear rather exposed when discussing these politically sensitive concepts. *The Shorter Oxford Dictionary* defines capitalism as

> 'The condition of possessing capital or using it for production; a system of society based on this; dominance of private capital.'

However in its Russian edition the same dictionary reads

> 'an economic and social system based on private ownership of the means of production, operated for private profit, and on the exploitation of man by man.'

The point of agreement between these definitions is that capitalism involves a whole socioeconomic system in which those who possess capital, dominate. It is for this reason we have studied the concrete outcome of capitalism with respect to the two contradictions we have examined. Socialism is defined by the same dictionary as

> 'A theory or policy of social organization which advocates the ownership or control of the means of production, capital, land, property, etc by the community as a whole, and their administration or distribution in the interests of all.'

As the 'success' of the capitalist system begins to undermine the ecological supports of life on this planet the phrase 'interests of all' begins to acquire new meaning. The neglected ideas, relating to the collective interest if developed within socialism, may begin to show new promise. This promise is yet to be realized in practice and it will not be realized unless a widespread and pervasive movement educates the majority about the changing nature of their interests and the indivisible quality of the problems facing humankind.

Schools
In schools the debate should be open and balanced. Our concern is that 'balanced' includes the perspectives represented in this volume.

So far they have been largely ignored. The 'contradiction in development' and the 'failure of success' within the capitalist system are issues which every educated person needs to confront and develop an intelligent opinion on. Our purpose in calling the conference on Education, Ecology and Development and in publishing the papers resulting from it, is to place before educators and interested members of the public some of the issues that must find their way into classrooms, lecture halls, newspapers, television programmes, political manifestos and future research. Perhaps in the future they may then be debated in board rooms, government offices, managers' offices and may result in a new sustainable relationship with our environment and our fellow inhabitants on the earth.

The process of research and publication into these issues has already led to some projects being set up by the World Wildlife Fund, OXFAM and other similar organizations. In addition, individual teachers and some schools have made pioneering attempts to introduce some of these topics into their curricula. However, in comparison with the massive redirection of resources that has been accomplished by the present government in order to give our education system a more vocational and skills based orientation, these efforts remain relatively small, uncoordinated and theoretically diverse. In the future the proposal for a 'National Curriculum' could lead to these pioneering attempts being snuffed out as the government and opposition parties compete with each other to promote short-term 'national interest' in terms of industrial and commercial relevance and vocational skills. This danger will only be averted if individuals, organizations and associations who begin to see the importance of the issues discussed in this volume work hard to coordinate their efforts and create a coherent philosophy for education. It will need to be a philosophy that unites a wide range of radical, socialist and ecological approaches. We hope that this volume will contribute in a practical way to the agenda.

References

Burke, J. (1985) *The Day the Universe Changed*. British Broadcasting Corporation, London.

Grant, J. (1987) *The State of the World's Children*. Oxford University Press.

World Bank (1984) *The World Development Report*. Oxford University Press.

PART ONE

INTRODUCTION TO PART ONE

Popular understanding about what is happening, therefore, is an urgent need. But how to achieve it? Information is being applied to the production side of the economy in a particular way, for private, corporate advantage. Yet it is also being applied to the human side. Here it is used to make people accept and believe that certain developments are benign, if not beneficial. It is applied to minimizing or deprecating opposition and to denying alternative options that might provide more humane direction.

Herbert Schiller
(*Information and the Crisis Economy*)

Few people would disagree with the notion that part of the purpose of education is to foster debate about, or at least bring into conversation, the value and validity of knowledge and understanding in connection with the major issues and concerns of the times in which they live. The growth of debate on environmental matters and the impact of human development processes on these matters is now being conducted worldwide at many levels of information and knowledge processing. The acquisition of knowledge and understanding confers power while the lack of it signifies the weakness of ignorance. In one sense, the papers in this book are about the management of ignorance by specific power structures in the global society through the denial of alternative understandings and particular perspectives and interpretations.

The call for Re-education

Such alternative understandings exist, but they are not generally part of the currency of educational exchanges in the curricula of schools and other educational institutions. Thus relevant or appropriate knowledge for alternative options is not necessarily included in what Bernard Lown describes as 'a direct purpose for education'. Lown (in Sivard, 1986) points to the obscenity of certain priorities that we espouse in terms of global military and social expenditure, where one hour's military spending would more than suffice to immunize the 3.5 million children destined to die annually from preventable infectious diseases. Lown asserts that

> 'People must be educated to understand the linkages between the arms race and global economic problems, as well as the deteriorating quality of their own lives. People must be made indignant at the subversion of technology and science.'

It would be possible to catalogue an array of priorities that support the viewpoints of both Schiller and Lown in their assessment of the ways in which 'understanding' and 'ignorance' are managed to support those particular systems of power and control that dominate the present global situation. It would also be possible to show that the direct purpose of education, as presently processed, excludes from its curricula and managerial arrangements opportunities to rectify the ignorance that disallows the consideration of alternative options. The reasons for this are, in part, historical, political, economic and cultural, and can be accredited to a view of the world in which the growth and power of the military/industrial complex and its modes of production requires a constant state of global emergency or crisis as being indispensable for its sustenance and levels of expenditure.

Ecological Problems and Re-education

Though the focus of this introduction has, so far, reflected a global dimension, it would not be too difficult to limit its range to a more localized sphere. Within regions, within states and within small communities there exist systems and structures which abuse and exploit human knowledge and human ignorance (in both the developed and the developing world). The challenge to education is not less demanding because of the presence of this differentiation of levels. Michael Redclift's paper, Chapter 1.1 ('Learning from the Environmental Crisis in the South') strongly asserts the international linkages between ecological problems and calls for a programme of re-education as to the nature and extent of 'environment' in the context of a developing country, and of appraisal of the contribution the developed countries make towards creating the ecological and development problems that the developing countries face. Complementing this perspective is John Abraham's paper, Chapter 1.2 ('Food, Development and Inner Ecology'). This paper threads together a series of different levels of concern, from the personal to the global, from an externalized ecology of the world to the inner ecology of the individual consumer. Both papers explore a range of dimensions and in doing so point to the pervasion of political and economic structures as effective agents in determining the ways and the means by which capitalism, as the most dominant world system, reifies its ideologies and principles through practices which create human as well as ecological problems.

Environmental Education and the Curriculum

In one sense Redclift and Abraham indicate major causes for concern as to the purpose and direction of the curricula of schools. One such cause for concern is to do with the lack of 'engagement' that most, if not all, curricular programmes display in regard to global problems of the kind that this book explores. This inability, or perhaps, lack of will, for engagement is analysed in David Pepper's paper, Chapter 1.3 ('The Bases of a Radical Curriculum in Environmental Education').

In this paper the concept of radical environmentalism is explored from political, societal and pedagogic standpoints. Within the framework of these interrelated positions, the interactions of social ideas and values and their concomitant political and economic structures, together with those of the environmental movement as it has evolved historically, are connected to the design and development of a curriculum for environmental education. The dominant features of such a curriculum are both radical and alternative and as such mark out clearly the distinction between it and the general purposes of the curricula currently implemented in schools, not only in terms of knowledge, but also in approach and methods. Pepper's paper reinforces the view of the role and function of environmental education as expressed in the general report of the Tbilisi Conference 1977, as being holistic in its approach to global problems, and therefore, interdisciplinary in methodology, innovative in creative processes, and, perhaps most importantly, renovative of educational systems as a whole.

As a conclusion to the introduction of Part One, I want to return to the quotation of Herbert Schiller. 'Popular understanding', in the fullest interpretation of the phrase, of current ecological and social systems, must be the direct purpose of the educational process if people are not to be manipulated and controlled into believing or accepting that the way the world is ordered at present is the only possible way and the way that it should or must go in the future. Other papers in the book, in various degrees and ways, offer critiques of a political and economic system which in ideology and practice despoils, degrades and even destroys the natural environments upon which we totally depend. Additionally, this system fragments and fractures human relationships to the detriment, misery and suffering of millions of people. The rational, if not the ethical, response to this programme of absurdity must be to examine and re-examine the causal relationship between the dominant systems and structures which govern human societies and their behaviour and the state of the world as it now exists.

Educational systems cannot be exempted from this process of examination. Alternative options based upon alternative philosophies and interpretations, must be considered and criticized. The imbalances in philosophy, theory and practice that characterize many educational systems are not immutable but they need to be redressed by the challenge of radical alternatives. To begin this redress has been the direct purpose of Part One of the book. While the viewpoint propounded is polemical, in terms of a particular political and ideological position, the aim is not one of solely presenting an alternative propaganda. Rather, it seeks initially to open up the agenda for discussion, and, eventually, to reconstruct the education systems, as the means for giving a more humane and ecological direction to the consequences of the human/ environment relationship.

References

Sivard, R.L. *World Military and Social Expenditures 1986*. World Priorities, Washington.

Schiller, H.I. (1986) *Information and the Crisis Economy*. Oxford University Press, New York.

Chapter 1.1

LEARNING FROM THE 'ENVIRONMENTAL CRISIS' IN THE SOUTH

Michael Redclift,
Department of Environmental Studies,
Wye College and Institute of Latin American Studies,
University of London

One day last autumn, 22 September to be exact, I was sitting on a bench outside a pub in the Derbyshire Peak District. I had been attending a meeting at the Peak National Park Study Centre in Castleton and this was the first opportunity to take in the delights of rural Derbyshire. Sitting next to me was an elderly man, Fred and his nephew, Stephen, both of whom spent almost every Sunday cycling around the National Park. They had, in fact, spent almost all their spare time on bicycles in the National Park during the previous 20 years. Fred had even been a member of the Clarion Cycling Club in the 1930s.

As we talked it became clear to both of them that I was as ignorant of the area as they were knowledgeable. 'You mean to say you don't know the National Park', said Fred, 'You've never been here before?' I confirmed that this was my first visit. 'Well', he asked, 'what is there down your way in Kent, then?' I replied that we were a bit short on National Parks – even access to footpaths in the countryside was very limited. 'Well,' said Fred, with a heavy sigh, 'You must have visited a National Park somewhere!' Feeling hopelessly unable to appear both normal and reasonably well-travelled I searched my memory for National Parks that I had visited, but none came immediately to mind. Just as I was about to admit defeat I realized that, yes, I had spent some time in a National Park. I had spent a month in the Bolivian Amazon in December 1984, much of it visiting colonization settlements, being dropped by aeroplane three or four hundred miles inside the green canopy. That was a National Park, so I told Fred and Stephen about it. Oh, the innocence of the over-educated! 'The Amazon, well if that's a National Park I'm a head-hunter!' said Fred. And, fortunately for me, we all decided to take the conversation in a different direction, finding an escape route in the beer and the weather.

This anecdote is recalled, for the first and last time I hope, to make a simple point that had not been clear to me at the time. When we say that ecological problems in the South are *our* problems as well as *theirs*, we are really prescribing for ourselves a programme of re-education, of relearning. To begin to re-educate we need first to unlearn, or at least to acknowledge that compartmentalizing 'environmental' problems has contributed to many of today's mistakes, and little to the solution of today's problems. We need to begin by clarifying the nature of the 'environmental crisis' in the South, and its relationship with our ideological assumptions. We need to bring Fred, and ourselves, into the picture.

There are three essential steps in explaining the nature of the environmental 'crisis' in the South:

1. We need to re-examine what we mean by the 'environment' in the context of developing countries.

2. We need to be clearer about the relationship between environmental problems in developing countries and the role of developed countries in their creation.

3. We need to re-examine the methods that are used for planning or 'managing' the environment in developing countries.

There has been an increased interest in the environmental problems of developing countries, particularly since the Stockholm Conference in 1972. Reports like the *World Conservation Strategy* (1980) and collaborative research like UNESCO's *Man and the Biosphere* (MAB) programme have drawn attention to the gravity of the situation in the South. We are much better informed than we were about the symptoms of environmental degradation, following the extensive documentation of the 'eco-crisis' in 'less developed' countries (LDCs) (Brown, 1984). In addition, attempts to 'model' the outcomes of environmental degradation have increased in sophistication (Global 2000, 1982). Public attention has been drawn to the environmental 'crisis' through the medium of television, video and print journalism. Non-governmental agencies like Oxfam and War on Want have emphasized in their development work the role of sustainable resource uses as a solution to environmental problems. Not least, government and inter-government agencies have been created to tackle these problems. The number of countries with government departments dealing with environmental management has grown from 15 in 1972 to 115 in 1980 (*World Conservation Strategy* (WCS) *UK*, 1983).

There is, then, no lack of attention paid to the Third World's environmental problems. Why do they remain and, in most cases, assume greater proportions? The answer to this question lies partly in the *way* environmental problems are identified and partly in the *means* that are required to deal effectively with them. Redefining the environmental crisis in the South is a first step towards effective action – whether on the part of political organizations, voluntary bodies in the developed countries, governments or international agencies. But it is not a sufficient step.

The Social Construction of the Environment

Most of the time we regard the environment as anything but *socially* constructed. Nature remains a bastion against society.

First, when we refer to 'the environment' in developing countries we are referring to something which has been produced by history, through struggles and exploitation, usually as part of the colonial and post-colonial accumulation process. Only when we refer to 'natural' wilderness is the colonial imprint relatively unimportant – and wilderness areas, especially in the humid tropics, are increasingly penetrated by metropolitan capital today. It is important not to divorce the environment from its parts, especially the human populations whose productive activities have contributed to its evolution.

Second, most pre-capitalist small-scale societies depend upon good environmental management to ensure future production. For hunters and gatherers, slash and burn cultivation and most 'peasant' or pastoralist groups, the viability of the natural environment is a condition of their existence. There is no divorce between their 'culture' and their ecology; Nature as a social category assumes importance in their very cosmology, their 'world view'. Their environmental practices *are* their cultural practices.

Third, the impact of capitalism in peripheral 'less developed' countries implies contradictions for those with limited access to resources and power. On the one hand the 'development' process brings them closer to the market, encourages the production of commodities and the sale of their labour for cash. On the other hand survival on any other terms becomes precarious. Self-sufficiency in food production or energy is difficult when labour, especially that of women, has to be allocated to gaining cash or to meeting the exigencies of the market and the state. Under these circumstances poor people inevitably have greater recourse to their environment – which acts as the focus of the household's attempt to reconcile the needs of the family with those of the market. Sometimes the only avenue of escape is migration – to the cities or 'across the border'. At other times no such safety valve exists, and environmental degradation ensues, as we have seen in the Sahel and Ethiopia. Where the natural resource base permits it, as in tropical 'frontier' areas such as the Amazon, households struggle with the environment, wresting control from nature and assuming a critical role in the process of gradual land concentration. Class struggles exist, but they are mediated by the environment. As those who accumulate wealth dispossess others, they are relocated to 'new' frontiers or return to work as wage-labourers within export-oriented, capitalist production. In relatively rare instances social struggles are undertaken in defence of the environment, as in the Chipko movement in India, where Hindu people adopted tree conservation as a last-ditch attempt to forestall external threats to their woodlands.

Underdevelopment and the Environment

The picture is often a confused one, and environmentally-minded individuals are unlikely to find in Third World situations an unequivocal commitment to environmental goals. Most of those who are blamed for causing environmental problems, especially the rural poor, are inarticulate and powerless. They seldom have the support of middle-class activists or a media committed to publicize their case. Conservationists frequently regard them with disfavour, as a threat to other species and to their habitat. A holistic concern with what impoverishes environments reveals the role played by international capital, trade relations and high technology agriculture. But this concern meets with ideological objections from most wealthy people in developing countries, who have a considerable stake in the development process. In addition, environmental problems suffer from 'reductionism' – if we seek explanations at a sufficiently local, 'micro' level it *is* the rural poor who often destroy the environment.

In most cases the poor are not only blamed for environmental degradation, they are the losers by it. People are brought into opposition with their environments in attempts to provide household necessities or finance deficit budgets. Those who control better land resources make greater use of chemical inputs and mechanical traction. The struggle for livelihood – which characterizes most interaction with the environment in developing countries – becomes increasingly dependent on inappropriate technological 'fixes'. As environmental degradation proceeds, through deforestation, desertification or the salinization of irrigation systems, indigenous knowledge is lost. It becomes more difficult to see the relevance of practices designed to ensure sustainable future production when the agricultural credit bank is leaning heavily on you today. In extreme cases, where the environment offers no hope of a solution, indigenous knowledge is simply irrelevant. This is the case in many areas of Africa today where pastoralism has declined in the face of the combined effects of governmental antipathy, urban policy bias, export cash cropping and severe drought. It is not the effect of economic, structural policies alone which accounts for the human casualties of environmental degradation, but it is not 'natural' disasters either. It is a potent combination of structural and environmental factors.

International Dimensions

The environmental problems of developing countries are clearly linked to their insertion within the international economy. It is important to remember, however, that this insertion has an historical dimension and that we cannot reduce the problem of specific geographical environments to contemporary economic and political relations alone. We also need to understand the objectives of developing countries, and their ruling elites, as well as the way in which pursuing these objectives meets obstacles – and encouragement – from the international economic community, especially the industrial states making up the Organisation for Economic Cooperation and Development (OECD).

Most developing countries in the Southern hemisphere are interested in securing some sort of industrial base, at the very minimum, one which would assist the development of their rural sectors. However, the level of industrialization achieved in the United States of America, Europe and Japan lies outside the reach of countries in the South, even those in Latin America which partially industrialized during and after the Second World War. Two immediate issues need to be considered: are less developed countries (LDCs) *allowed* to develop in the way they would like, given the interest of the developed countries in securing cheap raw materials and foodstuffs from the South? Also, do the resources exist in LDCs for a 'development' process which emulates, or replicates, the 'successful' development of the North?

Both these questions have clear implications for those interested in a political economy of the environment. It has proved impossible to shift the balance of advantage in trading relations or investment, from the countries of the North to those of the South via UNCTAD

(United Nations Commission on Trade and Development) and similar multilateral agreements. Even the Brandt Report, which proposed modest reforms in North-South economic relations met with few practical responses from the developed countries. As long as most LDCs remain poor and, in many cases, heavily indebted to the North, their development efforts will inevitably, take a heavy toll of long-term environmental factors in the quest for short-term economic 'benefits'. Cash crops will continue to be grown for the developed country markets; cattle will be reared extensively – often on land with rich arable potential; insecticides will be used without proper precautions; industrial pollution controls will be almost non-existent. Countries like Nicaragua that can ill-afford to ship a valuable resource like cotton in an unprocessed form, will continue to be forced to do so. In an analogous structural situation, that of Guatemala, it has been estimated that of the US$40,000,000 per year earned from cotton exports, about three quarters of that sum left the country in the form of purchases of pesticides, spray planes, tractors, etc, used as 'inputs' for growing cotton in a capital-intensive way. The *net* income from Guatemala from cotton exports was therefore only a quarter of what it appears to have been (Farvar, 1976).

If we assumed a different role for Guatemala in the international division of labour, cotton, instead of being sold raw, would be processed into thread, converted to cloth and made into shirts and other clothes. These would then be sold on the international market, creating domestic employment in the process. If we then asked, 'how much land devoted to cotton would be needed to earn the same amount of foreign exchange?' the answer is – rather less than one per cent of the land actually devoted to it! This case, which illustrates the structural constraints under which LDCs use their natural resources, also points to the close relationship between international economic relations and domestic land use and employment. The resources *do* exist for a more integrated form of development within many of the countries of the South, but they imply radically different trading and investment relations with the countries of the North.

It is still necessary to ask whether 'limits to growth' exist, but important to emphasize that these limits have a great deal to do with existing North-South economic relations. Demographic pressures on land and water resources exist in many LDCs, of course, propelling many of them to the edge of ecocatastrophe. But these pressures make sense only within the framework of international capitalism, in which poor countries provide supplies of raw materials and labour at market prices clearly beneficial to the rich. These global distributive issues are central to an understanding of every facet of the environmental problem – water supplies, soil erosion, food security, energy production and technological transfer.

Another aspect of the international situation which needs to be considered in the role of international organizations is the elaboration and implementation of environmental policy. There are a number of international organizations with a specifically 'environmental' brief. These include the International Union for the Conservation of Nature and Natural Resources (IUCN) founded in 1948, the World Wildlife Fund formed in 1961, organizations of the Council of Europe with responsibilities towards the environment and the United Nations Environment Programme (UNEP) formed after the Stockholm Conference in 1972. Most international organizations have a research or, at best, an advisory role, in international environmental policy. UNEP, for example, has the role of environmental monitoring, environmental planning and the dissemination of information. Its role has always been widely misunderstood, however. It is not a UN *executive* agency, empowered to carry out its own programmes in the member states (like the Food and Agriculture Organisation (FAO) or UNESCO). Nor is it a sprawling UN organization with a huge professional staff and a correspondingly large budget. Most importantly, UNEP is not responsible for most of the world's environment, most of which lies within the boundaries of sovereign nations which disallow interference from UN bodies in their international affairs (WCS-UK, 1983). The role of UNEP is to be a catalyst within the corridors of international opinion, raising consciousness of environmental issues especially within the UN 'system'.

The reality is that UNEP has little money and few staff, even fewer incentives to offer and no means of enforcing its wishes. It is a little like creating the UK's Natural Environment Research Council (NERC) without pooling the financial resources of its constituent member organizations and without coordinating their management structure (WCS-UK, 1983). Even the official document which was produced as Britain's contribution to the debate initiated by the *World Conservation Strategy* had this to say about UNEP:

At the end of the day, the unavoidable truth is that the combined resources of the Governments who came together at Stockholm to create the UN Environment Programme have simply not:
  (a) funded the Programme adequately;
  (b) cooperated with it adequately;
  (c) intervened with sufficient vigour to improve its performance;

(d) taken much notice of it (as Governments) except when it suited their short-term ends.'

(WCS-UK 1983, p.335)

Technology and Environmental Control

In the last decade or so the view has often been expressed that the logic of environmental politics lay primarily in planning. The following is a representative example of this position:

No goal is more central to the environmental movement or more politically contentious than comprehensive environmental planning. If one looks upon current environmental policy struggles for a sign or portent of the future direction of environmental politics, the quest for planning appears constantly ... as a common objective.

(Rosenbaum 1973, p.252)

The author of this book goes on to cite four 'fears' that LDCs have about the transfer of environmental planning from the North to the South. These are:

1. the fear of 'neoprotectionism',
2. the fear that attention to ecology might divert foreign aid funds,
3. the fear of environmental chauvinism in the conditions that need to be satisfied to receive aid, and
4. fear of the cost of non-polluting technologies.

These fears certainly exist, and they reflect the enormous difficulty in reconciling even modest development aspirations with global conservation goals and environmental management within LDCs. However, an even greater threat is represented by international agencies in the development field which act in concert with transnational corporations and governments to undermine environmental sustainability in the South.

One example is the 'Industry Cooperative Programme' (ICP), a group of over one hundred multinational agribusinesses that were housed in the FAO in Rome until 1978, and which influenced FAO policies in favour of their private interests. Their objective was to make agricultural development more dependent on inputs such as 'improved' seeds, agricultural machinery and agrochemicals. These inputs are sold and patented by these same companies (Farvar and Glaeser, 1979). Although the ICP was finally thrown out of FAO under the pressure of public exposure from writers like Susan George and the late Professor Eric Jacoby, corporate influence continues to be brought to bear on international agencies, most notably the United Nations Development Programme (UNDP).

Changes in agricultural technology, especially the development of chemical and biotechnology have enormous implications for LDC environments. Chemical-energy inputs are more divisible and less 'lumpy' than mechanical technologies and, in the form of new 'high yielding varieties' of rice and wheat, played an important part in the 'Green Revolution' of the 1960s and 1970s. They are also operated from outside the farms, and sold in 'packages'. The interest of large-scale capital lies in both selling the package and transforming the product. It is the stage at which the product is transformed that most profit is made, when the 'value added' to raw food production is included. Currently, in the countries of the European Economic Community (EEC) the price paid by consumers for food is, on average, three times that paid to the farmers. One should not forget, either, that the price paid to the farmers in the EEC countries is heavily subsidized!

Recent changes in the agro-industrial complexes of the North suggest several trends with consequences for LDC environments. First, the role of labour in agriculture in the future will be dictated increasingly by technological developments in the industrial sector. Biotechnology, for example, has been developed by venture capital, but has already outgrown this stage of its development. Already, agrochemical firms are buying their way into biotechnology, partly as a result of growing concentration in the agrochemical sectors (Buttel *et al*, 1983). These firms have merged with, or acquired, seed companies, the large, diversified 'deep pocket' transnational corporations that are well established in the seed industry supplying the South. The oil, chemical and pharmaceutical industries need to expand into seeds if they are to translate biotechnological potential into commercial success. The solution is to sell the farmer seeds which have their own built-in, bioengineered performance and need to be monitored and controlled from outside.

The role of the agro-industrial complexes in the North is important to developing countries in a number of ways, not least in their impact on the environment. Decision-making increasingly rests with people other than the farmer, while the poor farmer's lack of access to new technology may marginalize him further. By 'controlling' the natural environment in which agricultural production takes place, new technologies offer the possibility of transforming natural resources. This technical process rests, in fact, on the concentration of capital and technology in the hands of fewer people. The external effects, in surrounding areas through water and soil pollution, are often carried far afield. In some cases there is an observable loss in the diversity of local species and ecological sustainability.

The effects of these technological developments on LDC environments vary considerably. The lack of 'fit' between ecological systems and the technologies being introduced into the humid tropical areas of the South is discussed by Norgaard (1984). He lists four main characteristics of the Amazon ecosystem: enormous species diversity, a highly specialized system of nutrient recycling, uncertain succession responses in the biomass and rapid rates of growth of the biomass. Given these characteristics a compatible social system would be one with the following characteristics.

1. It would need to be a social system producing a variety of products for the regional market, often at a near-subsistence level.
2. It should involve the participation of native people using indigenous knowledge.
3. The social system should utilize technologies that were evolved in the tropics.
4. There should be the opportunity for formal and informal risk sharing.
5. Decision-making power should rest with the people managing the ecosystem.

What has happened in the Brazilian Amazon bears little relationship to this. Attempts have been made to introduce technological changes which enable more crops to be grown for distant markets and more labour to be transplanted from areas such as the poor North-East of Brazil. These technologies were developed in the temperate zone, not in the tropics. Finally, decision-making power usually rests not with local people in command of their environments but with government bureaucracies and large corporations in Brazil's developed region, the Centre-South and the developed countries. The social system that corresponds to the technological 'implants' is essentially incompatible with the ecology of the area.

The results are not difficult to predict, and can be observed in other similar humid tropical areas (Ewell and Poleman, 1980). The transnational corporations leave when the development subsidies have run out and the soils have been depleted. The peasant farmers revert to a multicropping farming system, providing food crops for personal consumption and a way of spreading risks. Such a system resembles slash and burn agriculture, which, combined with hunting and gathering, is precisely the pattern of farming developed by the original, indigenous, population of the tropical forests, to ensure a resumption in the fertility levels of the vulnerable soils and to provide time for a regrowth of the biomass. For such indigenous people environmental sustainability is a condition of agricultural production, rather than an alternative to it. Finally, the social cost in the degeneration of the colonizers' communities should be considered as part of the environmental cost of this type of 'development'. Despite the heavy cost of expensive infrastructure in areas of tropical expansion, most of the population remains vulnerable to disease and has little access to social services or regular employment. Once again forms of 'development' have been promoted without attention to even middle-term environmental and social effects.

Environmental Managerialism

The problems which an LDC faces in trying to develop a sustainable environment are not confined to transnational corporations and domestic elites. Transnational corporations can sometimes be 'kept out', perhaps through multinational action by LDCs organized for the purpose. Ruling classes are themselves 'dependent' on the economic relationships that exist with the developed countries; if these relations are radically changed it will unsettle domestic elites as well. The third obstacle in the way of 'ecodevelopment' is in some ways more intractable, and concerns the way environmental planning and management have evolved from developed country experience.

Consider the three main objectives of the *World Conservation Strategy* (1980). They were:

1. The maintenance of essential ecological processes.
2. The preservation of genetic diversity, and
3. Sustainable utilization.

Although these are eminently 'ecological' objectives, which raise few objections from advocates of different theoretical positions on development, the implications of trying to achieve them are more radical than is usually admitted. Outside the framework of the 'biosphere reserve', an area of land which is protected because of its environmental quality, achieving each of the three objectives requires concerted political action of a type not commonly found. In the face of the combined effect of accelerating demographic growth, increasing market penetration and urban 'bias', an 'ecodevelopment' orientation implies redirecting the development process in rural areas of LDCs. How far does current intervention, designed to achieve environmental objectives – what I shall term 'environmental managerialism' – provide a workable alternative to progressive environmental degradation?

There are various components of environmental management as practised in the South today. Most of them have been distilled from developed country experiences of conservation and planning, experiences which relate to industrial and 'post-industrial' societies, rather than underdeveloped countries. For example, the problems of environmental conservation in developed countries are bound up with food surpluses rather than food deficits, hence environmental planning is more closely related to the management of agricultural contraction than rapid agricultural growth. The value of amenity uses and aesthetic considerations loom large in the environmental movements of developed countries, while they scarcely figure among the priorities of people in the South.

The central tenet of environmental assessment is that there is an optimum balance of natural resource uses, which can combine sustainability in agriculture, forestry and other activities such as recreation. To establish the environmental interests which need to be considered it is necessary to undertake an evaluation of resource potential. Land use planning is a key technique in this approach, but land capability is not considered alone. Procedures have been developed for cataloguing lists of species, conducting soil surveys and establishing conservation priorities. Planning controls are then used on 'designated areas', to ensure that activities in these areas conform with overarching conservation and planning objectives.

The armoury of environmental management has been augmented in recent years by the inclusion of methods for social and economic appraisal. The projected cost of environmental losses can be assessed over an extended period, subject to the need to maintain an agreed level of ecological diversity. The emphasis in using cost/benefit analysis, environmental impact assessment and other socio-economic planning 'tools' is very much on measurability and quantification. As in the sphere of technological appraisal in the natural sciences, it is *techniques* which are evaluated, not policies, still less their implementation. Just as the underlying assumption of environmental assessment is that there is an optimum 'balance' of resource uses, the underlying assumption of environmental management is that long-term political interests in the environment are convergent. Sustainable development – unlike almost any other sphere of human activity – can be achieved through seeking consensus rather than conflict.

There are a number of objections to 'environmental managerialism' as set out above. First, the environment is usually only considered *after* the 'development objectives' have been set. The environmental aspects of a development situation are thus separated from the other aspects, often including economic and social factors. Furthermore, since very few projects undertaken in LDCs are *primarily* 'environmental' in scope, 'development' objectives completely obscure any other objectives. For example, in the 1970s in only 8 per cent of World Bank supported projects were environmental factors considered sufficiently serious to require the use of outside consultants (IBRD, 1979). In the majority of cases the costs of employing environmental assessment were less than 5 per cent of the total project cost.

There are wider implications of environmental managerialism as well. We are accustomed to regarding access to the environment ('countryside' in UK) as a means of escaping from social control, whether it is friends, kin, neighbours or daily routine. Part of the environment's legitimacy in 'post-industrial' societies, and the consensus about its importance, stems from its importance as a 'safety-valve' on the margins of urban life. In most LDCs promoting conservation objectives implies much more interference with poor rural people, whose environmental activities are designed to secure a livelihood rather than profit. Environmental management is a means of enforcing social control, not a means of escaping it.

Finally, and most importantly, environmental managerialism takes as a 'given' the distributive consequences which market processes and state power produce in the course of development. By divorcing 'environmental' from other distributive objectives, environmental managerialism helps to ensure that those who are well placed to avoid contact with the planning machinery do so, while those who are closest to the most severe environmental problems (desertification, deforestation, water contamination etc) are most likely to be uprooted and relocated. By locating the structural problems of underdevelopment in geographical space, usually in areas inhabited by the poor, environmental managerialism does not raise distributive issues in the development agenda, but serves to obscure them behind technocratic 'solutions'.

An Example: Environmental Management in Mexico

Environmental problems have characteristics which make for relatively easy diagnosis but difficult solutions. Among the difficulties encountered is the complexity of different variables in the pattern of 'causation'. Thus, agencies which wish to duck responsibility for environmental policy can usually cite a confusion of evidence about causal factors.

In addition, most environmental intervention has to be undertaken within inappropriate time horizons. It is impossible to evaluate most environmental interventions within a time frame of a few months. It is also difficult to implement environmental policy in a brief period. These difficulties affect radical socialist governments as much, if not more, than conservative ones.

Finally, it is difficult to establish clear 'environmental' parameters and to measure the effects of changes in food systems, for example, on the natural environment. It is not unknown for government delegations to arrive at international conferences on the environment, declaring that in their country 'environmental problems are secondary to problems of food production, water supply and infant health'! Fortunately, such curious platitudes are increasingly subjected to the criticisms of environmental activists within the Third World (Redclift, 1986).

The diagram in Figure 1 represents some of these issues for one country, Mexico. In the first column the national plans and programmes with some 'environmental' content are listed. In the second column the environmental components of these plans are specified. The column below these refers to the implementation of these plans.

Several conclusions emerge from an exercise of this sort. Clearly different plans carry contradictory implications for the environment. In some cases economic growth is the objective, in others it is amenity or conservation. Furthermore, these contradictions are present within sectorally-defined planning activities, as well as between them. The plan for agriculture, for example, seeks to promote a continuing increase in agricultural growth *and* the conservation of renewable natural resources.

Many environmental problems, of course, are inter-sectoral in nature, and shared between different ministries and government departments. Environmental programmes are also under-funded, undefined and scarcely ever properly evaluated. Where measures exist in law to prevent environmental damage (from pollution for example) the agencies whose responsibility it is to ensure enforcement usually lack professionally qualified people and political muscle. There is neither the expertise nor the political backing for decisive action on environmental degradation. Much public sector policy implementation in poor countries is heavily dependent on political bribes, not merely as a means of buying electoral support, but often simply as a way of disbursing funds which would otherwise remain unspent (and eventually 'returned' to central government). The benefits to be derived from implementing environmental measures are often relatively intangible, while the

Figure 1   *Environmental Management in Mexico (1984)*

Plans and development programmes	Environmental components of plan
1. Global development plan	– reduce pollution
2. National programme for agriculture and forestry	– conserve renewable natural resources
3. National plan for tourism	– maintain 'nature' for human access
4. National plan for urban development	– to develop natural resources for human settlements
5. Energy programme	– to protect the environment from energy growth (especially petro-chemicals)
6. Urban development for federal district (DF)	– to reduce urban pollution
7. Others eg, plans for agro-industry, fisheries industry, education, cooperatives, housing, science and technology	

Implementation
● Different plans often have contradictory implications for the environment, eg, the agricultural development plan (2) is geared to incremental growth, the energy (5) and tourist plans (3) imply reductions in growth.
● Public administration of development plans is organized sectorally. Problems and solutions are inter-sectoral.
● No specific provision is made for environmental programmes within public expenditure budgets.
● The strategy and instruments for implementing the various environmental objectives remain undefined. No provision for environmental impact studies.
● Limited fiscal measures against polluters and few efforts to reduce pollution.
● 'Biosphere Reserves' established by CONACYT in Durango, Jalisco, Quintana Roo and Sonora incorporate local populations in conservation activities. These show great potential.

(**Source** – Information from Alejandro Toledo, *Como, Destruir el Paraiso*, Centro de Ecodesarrollo, Mexico City, 1985.)

financial advantages which public sector employees can gain from powerful economic interests opposed to environmental measures, are very real indeed.

Defining an Alternative Project: from Theory to Practice

An alternative to environmental 'managerialism' needs to address several questions that are never raised within the conventional approach. First, it is necessary to demythologize the view that environmental management is free from political bias. Political conflict is at the very centre of the environmental 'problem' and at the centre of attempts to devise solutions to it. Second, an alternative project clearly needs to specify the *context* of local resource conflicts. As Blaikie (1984) argues, environmental problems need to be contextualized: the alternative is an avid reductionism which ultimately holds the poor responsible for 'their' environment. Third, we need to specify the political resources available to different interests in the local environment, rejecting the idea that any 'optimum' solution can be implemented which is at variance with the interests of dominant classes, the state and the international economic context.

The 'environment' that is in the process of construction in LDCs today is separated from our own by underdevelopment. It is differently located, not simply in geographical terms, but in terms of its role in the development process. It follows that the 'environment' in LDCs is an arena for different social aspirations and material struggles. Most environmental struggles in LDC environments are concerned with the conflicts between the interests *in* the environment of emerging social classes. Our task is first, to understand these conflicts, and second, to develop alternative action capable of strengthening the position of those groups which favour popularly-managed, resource-sustainable solutions. Technical inputs will have a role in the search for solutions, but there is no 'technological fix' capable of regenerating the environment and resolving social and economic problems.

A start must be made with structural policies, in areas like prices, agricultural credit and fiscal incentives. At present these policies seldom advance the interests of the poor or their environments. The relationship between changes in structural policy and needed technological changes must be specified much more clearly. Where do they leave the environmental actors, the combatants on the rural stage?

In addition, an alternative project needs to take indigenous knowledge much more seriously than it is taken at present. If structural policies can be devised which allow the poor a larger stake in the management of their environment, then it is *they* who will have to do the managing. There are two reasons for this: they are the people who understand their own environments best and, ultimately, they are the only people in a position to implement sustainable development.

This raises other issues. Norgaard (1984b) has argued that indigenous knowledge

'uses an evolutionary epistemology in a world view that directly clashes with the epistemology of modern science and of modernization'.

The challenge is therefore to scientists and technologists as well as to policymakers and political leaders. The rewards of learning from other cultures' experiences of conservation are considerable, as McNeely and Pitt (1985) demonstrate. Efforts must be made to build this experience into environmental projects, rather as environmental impact assessment and cost/benefit analysis are built into projects today. It is also important to appreciate that indigenous knowledge is often lost in the course of severe environmental degradation. Anthropologists and others can play a role in ensuring that, like the 'raised bed' systems of Tenochtitlan, what is lost to history is not lost to humankind.

Environmental change has both a contemporary and an historical dimension. These dimensions are usually overlooked in the desire to profit from developed country experience by adopting a 'managerialist' approach to environmental problems. This 'managerialist' approach is partly the product of our (historical) view of Nature, and partly the product of regarding the environment as separated from the development process. When capital is dedicated to the transformation of nature, the social forces released are part of the process of environmental change. They need to be part of our analysis and part of the solution. They constitute the means of creating value and, potentially, of recreating democratic environmental politics. What is required today, especially from those who count themselves on 'the Left', is an alternative project which locates the 'management' of the environment within a broader, political economy approach. This alternative project must be adequate to conditions in the developed and the developing countries. It must be relevant to the generation which inherited today's environmental problems and which is prepared to 'run the world' to draw the attention of the world to them. There may be little that British educationalists can do to prevent the crisis deepening, but there are plenty of opportunities to learn from the crisis, and make the links which others refuse even to acknowledge.

References

Blaikie, P. (1984) *The Political Economy of Soil Erosion in Developing Countries*. Longman, London.

Brown, L. *et al* (1984) *State of the World*. W.W. Norton and Co, London.

Buttel, F. *et al* (1985) Biotechnology in the world agricultural systems. In *Cornell Rural Sociology Bulletin*. 144.

Diaz, B. (1963) *The Conquest of New Spain*. Penguin, London.

Ewell, P. and Poleman, T. (1980) *Uxpanapa: Agricultural Development in the Mexican Tropics*. Pergamon, Oxford.

Farvar, M.T. (1976) Interaction of Social and Ecological Systems. In W. Matthews (ed.) *Outer Limits and Human Needs: Resource and Environmental Issues of Development Strategies*. Dag Hammarskjold Foundation, Uppsala.

Farvar, M.T. and Glaeser, B. (1979) *Politics in Ecodevelopment – a Cart Before the Horse?* Science Centre, Berlin.

Flores Cano, E. (1981) *Origen y Desarrollo de los Problemas Agrarios de Mexico, (1500–1821)*, Ediciones Era, Mexico.

Gibson, Charles (1981) *Los Aztecas Bajo el Dominio Espanol*. Edicion Siglo XXI, Mexico.

Global 2000 Report to the President. (1982) Penguin, London.

International Bank for Reconstruction and Development (IBRD) (1979) *Environment and Development*, The World Bank, Washington D.C.

McNeely J. and Pitt, D. (eds.) (1984) *Culture and Conservation: the Human Dimension in Environmental Planning*. Croom Helm, London.

Morales, H.L. (1984) Chinampas and Integrated Farms: Learning from Rural Traditional Experience, in di Castri *et al*, *Ecology in Practice*. UNESCO.

Norgaard, R. (1984a) Coevolutionary agricultural development in *Economic Development and Cultural Change*, **32** (3).

Norgaard, R. (1984b) Traditional agricultural knowledge: past performance, future prospects and institutional implications. In *American Journal of Agricultural Economics*, **66** (5) pp.874-878.

PRUSDA (1984) *Comision Coordinadora Para el Desarollo Agropecuario del Distrito Federal*, Mexico.

Redclift, M.R. (1986) Mexico's Green Movement, *The Ecologist* (in press).

Rosenbaum, W. (1973) *The Politics of Environmental Concern*. Praeger, New York.

Sanchez de Carmona, L. (1984) Ecological Studies for Regional Planning in the Valley of Mexico, in F. di Castri *et al Ecology in Practice*. UNESCO.

Toledo, A. (1985) *Como Destruir el Paraiso*, Centro de Ecodesarrollo, Mexico City.

Toledo, V.M. *et al* (1981) Critica de la ecologia politica. In *Nexos*, 47, Mexico.

Wittfogel, K. (1981) *Oriental Despotism*, Random House, New York.

World Conservation Strategy (1980) International Union for Conservation of Nature (IUCN), Gland, Switzerland.

World Conservation Strategy: UK (1983) The Conservation and Development Programme for the United Kingdom. Kogan Page, London.

Chapter 1.2

FOOD, DEVELOPMENT AND OUR INNER ECOLOGY

John Abraham,
University of Sussex

Introduction

Food lies at the centre of a set of crucial ecological and development issues facing us on a worldwide scale. Providing food for the hungry in the Third World continues to raise questions about how agriculture should be developed and organized, both internationally and within regional boundaries. Simultaneously, diseases associated with the overconsumption of certain types of processed foods appear to be on the increase in Western industrialized countries. Nutritional and toxicological uncertainty about the effects of huge quantities of food additives on our inner ecology looms large.

None of these issues exists in a social or environmental vacuum. A whole range of economic, cultural and ecological relations bear on food production. In particular, what we learn about a society's food and agriculture policies can give us a powerful focus on judging its political values and priorities. For the duration of this chapter, then, I shall ask you to see many wider social relations through 'food glasses' (Collins, *et al*, 1982).

The purpose of this chapter is to lay out a few substantive issues within the themes of Third World development and the pollution of our inner ecology. Implicit in the term 'development' is some notion of progress. I shall try to show that before we can sensibly discuss the 'development' of humankind we must first recognize that at the present time humanity does not in real, as opposed to ideal, terms share a unity of common interest. In short, we must first ask: progress for whom? Following a consideration of this question we can discard some strategies and adopt others based on the criteria of a possible progress for humanity as a whole.

The term 'ecology' refers to the inter-relationship of organisms to their environment. I will be concerned with the inter-relationship of people to their environment in both the production and consumption of foods. This chapter is by no means a comprehensive survey of the relevant issues. The causes of famines, food aid, the Common Agricultural Policy and the study of intrahousehold nutrition in the Third World are just four controversial and important areas which I am not able to address here.

The Extent of Mass Hunger

The number of people in the Third World suffering from hunger can be estimated in different ways. Hungry people suffer diseases known to be related to the deficient amount of food they are eating. Thus the extent of such diseases like kwashiorkor (resulting from protein–calorie malnutrition) or xeropthalmia (due to vitamin A deficiency) is an indicator of the magnitude of hunger in particular parts of the world. We can also try to assess the extent of world hunger by surveying the amount of food consumed by peoples or the amount of food available in different regions of the world via studies of household consumptions and income distributions.

In *The Fourth World Food Survey* the Food and Agriculture Organisation (FAO, 1977) used 1.2 times the basal metabolic rate (BMR) as the minimal requirement for basic nourishment. The basal metabolic rate is simply the energy required for the organs of the body to function. However, the internal heating of the body also requires energy (hence the factor of 1.2). People need at least this amount of energy to live and, if nourished, obtain it by eating.

Of course, people are generally active in many ways and need much more energy than this to live a working life. Nevertheless, at least we can say that people receiving less than about 1.2 times their basal metabolic rate (which in different regions can vary from 1,500 to 1,630 calories per day) are most definitely hungry. Grigg (1986), has demonstrated that, using this indicator, we can estimate that between 1978 and 1980 no less than 535 million people in the world were hungry, that is, 17 per cent of the population of the Third World. In Bolivia and many parts of Africa the figure is closer to 40 per cent and that is still using the conservative indicator of the FAO. The most recent and authoritative estimates of undernutrition are provided by the FAO's *Fifth World Food Survey* (1985). On the basis of new evidence the FAO considered that the indicator 1.2 times BMR used in *The Fourth World Food Survey* might be too low. Hence the number of undernourished people was estimated using 1.4 BMR and found to be 494 million in the Third World (FAO; 1986, New Internationalist, 1987).

It is, in practice, almost impossible to give exact measures of the number of people chronically hungry at the present time but it is almost certain to be more than 494 million because people do not merely desire to live in a purely biological sense, they also desire a way of life. Consequently they use energy in ways which do not conserve their calorie intake for solely biological-survival functions. Some sources have claimed that as many as 1,373 million, or 71 per cent, of the Third World's peoples go hungry (Reutlinger and Selowsky, 1976), though a similar but later study put the figure at 65 per cent (Reutlinger and Alderman, 1980).

Even if we cannot be certain of the extent of hunger we can conclude that mass hunger is prevalent in the Third World and that many millions of people are starving. Although data have been collected in order to assess the numbers of hungry people since the 1950s, it was not until the World Food Conference of November 1974 in Rome that mass hunger became the focus of international attention. Since then mass hunger and malnutrition in the Third World has been dubbed 'the world food problem'. Unlike famines it is a chronic condition.

While we can find consensus about the existence of mass hunger, little agreement about how to alleviate it is forthcoming. The various 'solutions' which have been suggested tend to embrace different models of 'development', global resources and the environment. Two distinct approaches can be discerned. I shall call these the *aggregates approach* and the *structuralist approach*. The former sees the elimination of world hunger as resting on a food production/population equation but the latter considers it to rest on the transformation of various social, political and environmental conditions in which hungry people are located.

For those who focus their attention on aggregates, 'the world food problem' must be solved, either by reducing population growth (if not population) or, increasing food production in Third World countries. The applications of these two prescriptions has meant birth control programmes and 'Green Revolutions' respectively in the underdeveloped world. Crucial lessons can be learned from a critical appraisal of these policies.

Understanding Population Growth and Hunger

It is nearly 200 years ago since Malthus (1798) wrote that

'population, when unchecked, increases in a geometrical ratio. Subsistence increases only in an arithmetical ratio'.

Neo-Malthusians are particularly concerned about the problem of 'overpopulation' and especially the fact that in some parts of the world the aggregate population growth is outstripping aggregate measures in food production. This is a problem because, so we are told, it means there are too many people and not enough food to go round. In short, the neo-Malthusian claim is that 'overpopulation' helps cause hunger. Obviously such a claim has radical implications for development strategies against hunger.

We know about the past trends in population growth over the years due to the work of demographers. Demographers and futurologists often supplement their data collection with forecasts of how many people will live on the planet by a certain date. For example, approximately 4.7 billion people populate the earth at the present time and *The Limits To Growth* (Meadows, 1972) predicted that the world population would reach 8 billion by the year 2000. Two years later the first world population conference was held in Bucharest. In an interesting article, Tabah (1975) then the Director of the Population Division in the Department of Economic and Social Affairs of the United Nations (UN), illustrates the *aggregates approach*:

> 'In a world where population growth reaches 75 million a year, and will continue to do so for at least seven or eight decades, cereal production would have to be increased by about 30 million tons, ie by the equivalent of two thirds of the amount imported by the Third World in 1973, merely to maintain the present level of consumption which is already tragically low. Around the year 2000, when there will be about 6,400 million people to feed and an annual growth of 120 million, all else being equal, the deficit will have increased by some 70 per cent. For India alone, the annual population growth – around 12 million – demands an additional 5 million tons of cereals, ie almost half as much as the 10 million tons required for the Third World – which the Rome Conference has still not been able to find.'

Within this perspective population growth is seen as a threat. Indeed it is often referred to in very threatening language such as the 'population bomb' or the 'population explosion'. More people, we are told, drains the world's already depleted resources by making more demands on food production. Brown (1975), the president of the Worldwatch Institute which strongly subscribed to the *Global 2000 Report to the President* maintains that more people in the Third World threatens our ecosystems. According to this view, we must severely curb population growth in Third World countries in order to save the environment, especially forests and grasslands. This is because too many 'peasants' and shifting cultivators, so the argument goes, use more timber and land than can sustain the population in the long term.

Much more recent estimates of population trends have led some commentators to conclude that the 'global population crisis is over' (Pearce, 1984a). Such relief seems to follow the 1984 UN Population Conference in Mexico when the official UN figure for the world's population was projected at only 6.1 billion by the turn of the century. But even in 1984 population growth in Africa still outstripped food production in aggregate and so Africa was singled out as the continent of humanity which had to 'face up to overpopulation', with the possibility of having to support 900 million people by the year 2000 (Marshall, 1984). One report, however, suggests that food production in Africa rose by 3 per cent in 1986 outstripping population growth for the first time in 15 years (Hilsum, *The Guardian*, 1987). No doubt we can expect this to be followed by the identification of individual African nation-states where 'overpopulation' is promoted as the human threat.

There is an immense abundance of demographic statistics and predictions which can be quoted. It is not so much the predictions of an 'overcrowded' planet that we need to challenge if we are to understand hunger but rather the reasoning that lies behind the whole notion of 'overpopulation'.

The first thing we should realize is that the resources of the earth are easily enough to feed everyone on the planet. It has been estimated that using Western farming techniques of the 1980s the world's agricultural resources could muster enough food to feed adequately 33 billion people. Even using primitive farming methods which excluded fertilizers, pesticides and soil conservation pro-grammes the world population of the 1980s could be comfortably fed (Pearce, 1984b). Hence, we may conclude that a rational food production system organized to feed everyone could, in principle, be developed without any anxiety about population growth. This fact, in itself, suggests that people starve for reasons unrelated to their abundance.

The structuralist approach offers much more promising expla-nations. By taking such a perspective we are invited to consider that the structure of land holdings has far more to do with explaining hunger than total populations. China is generally credited with feeding almost, if not, all of its people, yet it is one of the most populous countries in the world with only 0.13 hectares per person (less than for most other countries in Asia). This figure is only one third the amount of land per person in Bangladesh where thousands are chronically hungry. The truth is that only the poor go hungry. In Bangladesh where 80 per cent of the population lives in rural areas many of these poor people are landless. They may rent land or they may be unemployed. George (1976) illustrates the point well when she points out that even though there are 326 people per square kilometre in Holland but only five in Bolivia, people are adequately fed in Holland but famines strike in Bolivia. Furthermore, we are not aware of anyone arguing that there is an 'overpopulation' problem in Holland. We can see that some people are well fed while others go hungry independently of the number of people in a country, region or continent.

While the poor go hungry it is also the rural poor who have large families in Third World countries. According to the 'overpopulation' theorists this is because those people lack the availability of birth control programmes, contraceptives and the education to see that they should limit their families in their own interests. Yet it is now recognized that family planning programmes with population targets, such as the five year plans in India, have been unsuccessful (Ledbetter, 1984).

Thanks partly to the pioneering work of Mamdani (1972), we know that this is because many villagers accepted contraceptives from family planning project workers to avoid causing trouble. The villagers told the family planners that they were taking the tablets when they were, in fact, throwing them away or in one case making sculptures with them! Advocates of population control often consider this kind of behaviour as evidence that the villagers need education to see the folly of their ways. However, Mamdani's research enables us to appreciate that the rural poor in Third World countries have real interests at stake when they decide to have more children. Where infant mortality is high and poverty is just around the corner more children represent 'free labour' and socioeconomic security for the future.

It is unfortunate that an understanding of the social causes of population growth had to await the failure of many extensive birth control policies throughout the world. Even if we ignore some of the disturbing reports of coercion associated with such policies (Hartmann and Standing, 1985, cf. Vines, 1985) it is depressing to find the 'overpopulation' thesis repeated with such regularity. However, we should not leave birth control without some consideration of China where there has been dramatic success.

The reasons for this success are almost as complex as the Chinese social system itself but we can identify the major factors involved. In the first instance mass involvement of the rural poor in collective agricultural activities is encouraged and rewarded. Land reforms have meant that extreme poverty and hunger have been eliminated so that the desperate economic need for children has been reduced. Nevertheless, the family is still of significant importance in Chinese society and the elderly look to their offspring for support in old age. In particular, sons are strongly preferred over daughters and in many cases Chinese parents will continue to have children until they have their first son.

Mosher (1982) provides us with a very illuminating account of the decision-making process involved in China's birth control policies. At the village level it is the job of the Women's Federation to explain the family planning regulations which called for couples to have no more than two children, spaced at least three years apart. In the village studied by Mosher an early consensus was reached by the peasants and the cadres (women members of the communist party delegated to oversee family planning at the village level) of the desirability of only two children per family. A major reason for this was declining child mortality rates. Families no longer had to have large families to sustain themselves. However, the cultural value of boys meant that for some peasants 'two children' became translated into 'two boys'. The cadres found that out of 1,500 families in the village, 74 women and their spouses did not conform to the regulations. After persuasion and mild disincentives, through meeting and discussion, 64 women remained unwilling to embark on any form of contraception. Most of these women were wanting to have either their first or second boy.

Clearly, family planning is not an unqualified success in China. What success there has been derives from the fact that Chinese peasants find themselves in a very different social system to that experienced by Indian peasants. Chinese communism means a more egalitarian and collective political system has been created before any birth control system. Having said this, the limited resistance to the family planning programmes arises because patriarchal culture remains powerful. The view that males are more important than females has not been effectively challenged beforehand. It is this failure to confront some of the underlying causes for the desire to have larger families which threatens the success and humanity of China's family planning.

We can see, then, that the reasons for population growth are social, cultural and economic as well as biological and that these dimensions of people's lives must be tackled first. But in the meantime what about the environment? Does an overabundance of 'peasants' cause too much deforestation and long-term damage to the ecosystems on which we will depend for future food? While we would be foolish not to share Brown's (1975) concerns for the degradation of the environment, we might hesitate to attribute the cause to 'population pressure'. Other viewpoints suggest that it is more correct to say that the demands of corporate capitalism are at the root of intense deforestation. (Plumwood and Routley, 1981–82). In recent times the tropical forests have seen their most rapid retreat since the 1960s. Although this is correlated in time with large population growth, we also know that this is the time when transnational companies began to have an impact on the postcolonial Third World. This corporate based influence whether in the area of forestry, agribusiness or construction can lead directly to large-scale deforestation of much greater proportions than subsistence farmers are likely to perpetrate. It can also be the reason why more subsistence farmers look to the forest for their land in the first place. In a country like Brazil where inequality of land ownership is acute, poor farmers and shifting cultivaters are not at the edges of the forest because there are too many of them but because they have been forced off their land. Poverty has forced them to sell their land so that they are able to feed themselves.

Once again we cannot properly understand why people reduce forest cover, any more than we can understand why they are hungry, by recourse to aggregates. This is not to suggest that population growth and deforestation are trivial or irrelevant matters to Third World development. We might wish for a world in which both were of lesser proportions but in doing so we must understand that such a world would afford very different social conditions to the peoples who actually form part of these very processes at the present time.

Patterns of Social Power and the 'Green Revolution'

Whilst population planners worried about increasing birth rates in the 1960s, geneticists were engaged in plant breeding experiments in Mexico. These scientists were attempting to produce synthetic seeds which would yield a greater wheat output than the traditionally known natural varieties. The Rockefeller Foundation had been supporting this type of research since the mid-1940s. Later similar research into rice varieties was undertaken. In the 1970s these plant breeding techniques were introduced into some of the agricultural systems of South-East Asia. This became known as the 'green revolution'.

For its supporters the 'green revolution' promised an overall increase in food production. The idea was that there would be more food to go round and so the hungry would be fed. For many it meant the modernization of inefficient traditional agriculture and the arrival of prosperous capitalist industrial agriculture. It could even be the capitalist solution to hunger and the high yielding varieties (HYVs) were often called 'miracle seeds'.

The implications of the 'green revolution' in many Third World regions are still extremely controversial and incompletely understood (Mars, 1978; Prahladachar, 1983) but we do know from the research of Griffin (1974), Bardhan (1970) and many others that the optimism of the early 1970s was largely unfounded. According to Griffin 'the story of the green revolution is a story of a revolution that failed'. We can learn a great deal about the problem of development against hunger and its relationships to social structures and the environment by examining this failure.

The advantage of the rice HYVs was that the plants were shorter and stockier than the traditional varieties which would keel over if a large amount of fertilizer was applied. So in laboratory conditions where precise amounts of fertilizer and water can be supplied the HYVs were much more impressive. However, an appreciation of their relationship with the rest of the environment and the ecosystems in which they were to be placed is clearly desirable. In the agricultural contexts of South-East Asia the HYVs were susceptible to floods (due to shortness) and could not always receive the required amount of water due to unavailable irrigation facilities. The HYVs were not resistant to pests and therefore regular doses of pesticides needed to be applied. Sometimes lack of foresight about environmental conditions simply meant that the crops could not survive. In some cases extensive use of pesticides can present a hazard to the ecological balance of the region. For example, there has been concern that DDT levels (along with other pollutants) in the oceans might increase to the point of seriously reducing the oxygen-producing phytoplankton or seriously interfere with the reproduction of major fish species. In other instances the persistence of the agrichemicals in the food system means that significant pesticide residues remain in the foods consumed by hungry children. These residues can represent acute or chronic toxic hazards (Bull, 1982).

It is now clear that the high yielding seeds require a whole package of complementary technologies in order to function in the environment. Hence only the richer farmers could afford to invest readily in the 'miracle seeds'. In particular, the politics of water control became very important. The wealthy landowners tended to control irrigation facilities and thus were able either to deny access or charge a fee for it. In this sense 'green revolution' technology was not scale-neutral as was commonly argued. Even where canal irrigation is controlled by the state, without the economic capacity to invest in tubewells and pumping devices, efficient application of the seeds, fertilizers and pesticides may not be possible. In a competitive situation such as India, Pakistan or the Philippines, efficient application of agricultural resources is crucial to the survival of small farmers. For this reason many small farmers felt the investment risk was too great while others lost out by adopting the technological package incompletely.

It follows that, relative to rich farmers, the poor smallholders were in a 'no win' situation with respect to adoption. As a result the 'green revolution' tended to exacerbate pre-existing inequalities in some Third World regions. Although the promise of a rise in overall food production was realized in many of these regions hunger was not reduced. Even though more food on the market pushed prices down small farmers often suffered a greater reduction in their incomes preventing them from buying as much food as before.

The picture is completed if we look at the effects on landlords. Some landlords, who had previously leased out their land, became enterprising capitalists committed to profit maximization once they realized how the new technologies could enhance the profitability of cultivation. With new found enthusiasm for agriculture landlords evicted tenants so that the land could be farmed. Although the labour intensive activities of fertilizer application and multiple cropping provided additional employment this was offset by evicted tenants and bankrupt smallholders looking for work. Even the labour generating aspects of the 'green revolution', such as increased demand for harvesting (some hybrid corns have achieved fifty-fold increases in yield) and threshing, are likely to be short-lived as big landowners begin to mechanize with labour displacing tractors and harvester combines. In regions like the Punjab unemployment and insecurity of work means poverty and the inability of people to purchase enough food. If we are serious about development against hunger in these regions then we desperately need to appreciate that hunger is due to poverty which is created by a competitive agricultural system built on massive inequalities of land and wealth.

In the long term people's poverty is not divorced from the poverty of the environment. This is why there is another regional and global implication of the 'green revolution' which we urgently need to debate, namely, the loss of genetic diversity associated with this type of plant breeding. The model of agriculture underlying the 'green revolution' is, as we have seen, one which favours those with plenty of capital. Large farmers have plenty of capital but so too do large companies.

The 'green revolution' has created a market for the HYVs which has radically changed the relationship of corporate capital to agriculture. The emphasis is on productivity through profitable 'plant packages'. This means that single crops are used in conjunction with huge amounts of agrichemicals some of whose ecological risks I have already mentioned. More striking is the fact that new plants are now designed to fit this chemical mould – sometimes together with the specific fertilizers and pesticides to be used.

Indeed to maintain this control over the plant market, fertilizer and pesticide companies are now trying to buy up seed companies. The ability to design, create and patent specific kinds of plants gives suppliers of plant varieties more control over what is grown, over the price at which seeds are sold and over the purpose for which crops are grown. This means that types of plants and their growing conditions are increasingly and rapidly being shaped by agribusiness. In return some of us will get food (Yoxen, 1983).

Today most of the food we eat in the West has its genetic origins in the Third World. The large numbers of strains of different crops in the Third World offers natural protection against lack of water (for example, through monsoon failures), crop disease and pests. Uniform seeds are more vulnerable to disease yet the agribusiness style of development is spreading seed conformity on a worldwide scale. Increasingly the seed companies draw on the Third World 'seed banks' in Mexico, Chile, Syria and El Salvador to keep one pace ahead of pests and plant disease. The result is genetic erosion and displacement with the consequent drying up of the 'seed banks'. As plant packages enter our food systems with their high levels of pesticide residues and other indirect food additives, our choice of food systems might well be dwindling before many people realize that such a choice needs to be made.

International Commodification of Food

At a regional level, changing some of the inequalities responsible for malnutrition is difficult in the face of powerfully entrenched capitalist and technological agrosystems. In addition, any nation wishing radically to change such systems, and thereby the direction of its food policies, cannot ignore international relations. We shall look closely at Cuba in the next section but first I want to explore some of the ways in which international capitalism affects some familiar foods.

We generally think of food as a basic need for survival. Nutritionists study how different foods and elements of foods provide (or fail to provide) us with nutrients which are vital to our daily lives. However, for the people able to control the international exchange of food products, food is a commodity. As a commodity within capitalism it is not the nutritional value of food that counts but its economic value. In short, its propensity to generate profit within a particular market is what counts to the capitalists.

We can see this by considering the international economic and political profiles of three everyday food products consumed in the

West – coffee, tea and meat. If you live in the West you will probably have tea or coffee every evening. Most of the time when you reach for your hot drinks you won't even think about their international origins or the economics of their price. Yet an appreciation of the process of transforming crops into food commodities for the market system is crucial to our understanding of many environmental and nutritional crises in Third World countries.

Coffee

Coffee was first grown in Ethiopia and, via the Amsterdam Botanic Gardens, was introduced into Brazil in the 18th Century. Coffee is now one of the most important commodities to enter international trade by virtue of its annual traded value of around £5,000 million (Clutterbuck and Lang, 1982). It has been estimated that some 20 million people work to produce it. Brazil exports several million tonnes, more than any other country. Consequently the Brazilian government keeps a close watch on the international coffee market. In the past if too much coffee was being produced worldwide, lowering the price on the market, the Brazilian government would, at times, destroy stocks. Then if there is a shortage, with prices rising sharply, the government would encourage rapid planting of new coffee trees, maybe up to 500 million new trees in several years.

Often the demands of the coffee plantations require extensive deforestation and the devastation of many species. Future fluctuations in prices may then lead to the running down of the plantation. Usually the land has not been prepared for other forms of agriculture and the soil is left open to erosion. The international competitive market situation means that at a later date coffee production will be stepped up to profit from high prices. But, it is very likely that the old plantation land is too eroded to be of any use, so new forest areas are cleared to accommodate the new plantation and the cycle restarts.

Of course, this crazy cycle is not designed to feed Brazilians. This amount of coffee would not be required to supply everyone in Brazil, even if large numbers did not go hungry. Indeed, the irony is that in 1977 Brazil was buying up coffee from Angola and El Salvador while withholding its own in order to maintain artificially high prices on the international market. In the very short term, the Brazilian government stands to gain a lot from such actions because coffee growers in Brazil are legally bound to pay a substantial proportion of their profits to the government's monopoly trading organization. For the same reason, farmers are encouraged to invest in monoculture coffee agriculture. Like monoculture HYVs, the coffee is then particularly open to disease and pest attack. In addition, this economistic domination of agriculture means that a great deal of indigenous farming knowledge is squandered.

Tea

In the case of tea a different story may be told but with a similar tune. The tea plantation economy in the Third World has many connections with British colonialism. Although Asian countries produce around 75 per cent of the world's tea, British or part-British firms trade around 70 per cent of it (North, 1986). Tea growing is dominated by Western firms.

Historically, imported tea changed the social habits of an entire class of Europeans during the 17th Century. Because tea was bulky and consumed in much larger quantities than spices, its production, like coffee, needed large plantations. One reason for this is the relative elasticity of demand for tea. That is, consumers' ability to consume tea (or coffee) is fairly unlimited, in comparison to potatoes, for example. This partly explains why tea produced in Africa increased sixfold between 1960 and 1980 (Lappe and Collins, 1982).

Another reason why tea companies make large profits is because of the extent of exploitation of labour involved. Exploitation of labour is, of course, a function of capitalism as much as profit itself, but there are varying degrees of exploitation within capitalist enterprises. In 1974 a World in Action television programme documented the horrendous living conditions of Sri Lankan tea pickers. Their payment of 36 cents per day is, unfortunately, not the lowest wage one can find for such work in the Third World. This kind of poverty leads to malnutrition, illness, inability to work, greater poverty and eventually chronic hunger.

Just from looking at coffee and tea we can see that the cultivation of cash crops constitutes a major part of Third World agriculture. One report suggests that an area about one and a half times the size of California is dedicated to this task (Tudge, 1979). This is more than enough land to feed all the world's hungry people yet it is used to produce foods of little or no nutritional value. Furthermore, in some areas such as Kenya and Tanzania there is substantial substitution of food crops with cash crops. This is partly due to government schemes designed to increase incentives for the development of cash crops which have not been extended to food crops.

Given that it is food crops rather than cash crops which enable Third World countries to feed their own peoples, why should Third World governments like Brazil, Kenya and Tanzania promote a cash crop economy? The answer to this question has many facets but we can gain some clues by appreciating that the interests of governments do not necessarily coincide with the interests of the rural poor.

Firstly, large companies, such as Nestlé or Brooke Bond, have teams of managers and lawyers whose job it is to consult with Third World governments. Using these resources the companies can promote their interests to governments and affect policy. Secondly, the capital flow received by Third World governments from their cash crop economy gives them bargaining chips to use in foreign exchange and a means by which to pay foreign debts. Even though cash cropping may be structurally crippling the agriculture in a Third World country the demands of the urban centres for luxury commodities can be too great to resist. Such an urban biased approach can aid government rhetoric that the country really is on the road to 'development'.

Meat
Similar principles apply to the branch of agribusiness concerned with satisfying the West's enormous appetite for meat. However, the meat business has a much more significant impact on food systems. Nutritionally valuable foods such as cereals and beans are fed to livestock causing a loss of around 90 per cent of the original vegetable protein. In the case of chicken, traditional food crops such as corn have given way to the chicken feed crop sorghum in Colombia. These activities place a tremendous nutritional burden on the Third World poor because the prices of staples and cheap sources of protein like beans are displaced by expensive meat sources.

Also, we should not underestimate how the beef sector of agribusiness is responsible for large scale changes in the environment. Slashing and burning of tropical forests followed by ranching on the forestland can have devastating effects on the soil and the lives of the indigenous people. As with coffee and tea this ranching is geared, not so much to produce nutritional food, but rather to fill the big retail outlets in the United States or Central American capitals with profitable commodities like hamburgers. In agribusiness exploitation of people and the environment go hand-in-hand.

So powerful are the international political and economic relations of food production that even when national governments try to implement non-capitalist alternatives to agribusiness they experience acute and perhaps chronic difficulties. Nevertheless, we can learn a lot about the relationship between food policy and development by studying alternative models of development.

Food Policy In Alternative Models of Development: Cuba

From the preceding sections it is clear that prepackaged solutions to Third World hunger within competitive capitalist social relations have little to do with feeding the rural poor. Furthermore, because of the commodification of food under international capitalism, food production in Third World countries can undermine the long-term capacity of the rural poor to feed themselves and farm their own environment. It follows from this that development against hunger in the Third World requires a change in the social relations of food production and a reformulation of the mechanisms by which Third World countries trade with the West.

Arguably, the revolutionary government of Cuba has tried to do this. How did Cuba make changes in food production? What implications for development more generally does the Cuban experience hold for us?

Before the 1959 revolution Cuba's economy was structurally 'dependent' on the US. There are many different theories of international dependency but in essence it is a dichotomous relationship between national economies resulting in the dependent nation responding primarily to foreign rather than domestic economic and political forces. In particular, structural dependence refers to the emergence of underdeveloped countries due to a dependent response to the demands of 'advanced' (usually capitalist) economies.

We can see that this definition is clearly satisfied by the pre 1959 US–Cuban relations since two-thirds of Cuba's trade was with the US and over half its sugar exports were aimed at the US market (Leogrande, 1978). In addition, under the Batista regime 1.5 per cent of landowners controlled over 46 per cent of all the farms in the country. Cuba was an acutely unequal society propped up by vast American interests. Immediately before 1959 the agricultural economy was monopolized by American owned cane and cattle shareholders and a few Cuban companies.

Of crucial significance is the concentration of resources on the cash crop, sugar. In 1958 sugar companies owned or controlled around 27 per cent of the total agricultural land in Cuba (Floyd, 1978). Cuba's dependence on the US explains the crazy paradox that, while the Caribbean country was a major exporter of raw sugar, it imported candy. Dependence on the US economy and cash crops, combined with internal inequalities, had two consequences:

1. A great deal of poverty, unemployment and the concomitant

food insecurity. The poor were forced to live on a few beans and cassava.

2. About two-thirds of Cuba's farmland went uncultivated and nearly half the total farm area was kept in pasture, unattended to. Large American-type ranches often used good farmland to graze an average of only two head per five acres. As a result staples such as rice, lard, vegetable oils, beans, potatoes, dairy products, eggs and vegetables which Cuba could have produced in abundance were imported.

(Benjamin *et al*, 1984)

The unquestionable success of the revolution in 1959 is that it has eliminated hunger in Cuba. This was achieved by major agrarian reform laws and food rationing. Agrarian reform involved the government buying up large expanses of agricultural land which then became state farms. The government also encouraged individual smallholders to become members of cooperatives by attaching various community services to membership. The clear message was that food should be produced collectively and for the benefit of all. The ethos of individualistic competition was discouraged. Most importantly, food rationing ensured that 'basic needs' such as rice, beans, oil, bread, sugar, meat, milk and salt were set at very cheap prices that everyone could afford. Other expensive foods can be bought on the parallel market or in restaurants. Both these are also controlled by the state to varying degrees.

The US trade embargo after the revolution meant that Cuba had to reconstruct a large part of its international relations. To achieve this, the revolutionary government in 1960 decided to try to diversify the agricultural sector by breaking the economy's dependence on sugar production, but at the same time to continue to ensure that no-one went without adequate food. Hence, the problem for the Cuban government was to increase food production selectively so as to meet the nutritional needs of the whole population without reliance on imports which had to be purchased with the foreign exchange gained from sugar exports. In short, Cuba was trying to become self-reliant in food. This has not been achieved and to this day Cuba depends on imports for much of the food basic to its diet (for example, over 80 per cent of beans are imported and about 40 per cent of rice). It is important that we pause to consider why.

It seems likely that one reason for this failure was a lack of consideration of the environmental preconditions for agrosystems in the planning stages. The model of development adopted by the Cuban government for agriculture was one of modernization through technological inputs. This has several implications for agrosystems. Clearing of the land was often done using heavy bulldozers which destroyed thin topsoils leading to severe erosion. Later, these areas were to have greatly reduced yields especially in bean production. The cutting back of sugar cane acreage, weedland and forest was not only expensive but other areas were more suitable for cultivation. Another problem with this model of development is that indigenous knowledge and understanding of the environment by local farmers tend to be undervalued. This seems especially pertinent to Cuba because the government set production targets without first exploring the different skills required by farmers in working the hi-tech agriculture compared with the traditional techniques. This meant that the required inputs in terms of seeds, fertilizers, pesticides and irrigation for the particular agrosystems in question were not understood. As Magdoff commented:

'... in most cases it is not the lack of fertilizers or use of poor varieties but rather inadequate agro-technique – soil preparation and management, weed and other pest control, irrigation timing and rates, etc. I doubt whether the current methods of experimentation at the farm level are really asking the right questions.'

(Magdoff, 1980)

In fact, there is some evidence to suggest that the remaining small private farms using more traditional farming methods provide greater yields than the large hi-tech state farms.

There are, however, other reasons for the failure of diversification in the early 1960s. In particular, the concentration of hi-tech agriculture also brought a renewed emphasis on mechanization yet many of the spare parts of Cuban tractors were of US origin. This was also true for the trucks needed to transport farm products to the markets. The trade embargo had a crippling effect in this respect.

In addition, redistribution of wealth and land gave many agricultural labourers the opportunity to alter their employment. This led to labour shortages on some farms. Low production figures in beans, cassava, citrus and dairy items were the result. The government's commitment to feed all the people could not be implemented without significant imports and that meant reverting to dependence on sugar – the current situation.

Could the failure to diversify have been avoided? It seems likely that it could but only with planning which integrated both the long and short term. One way of understanding Cuba's diversification attempt is through the opposing forces of short-term and long-term needs.

The short-term economic pressures and internal consumer pressures prevented the revolutionaries from achieving diversification even though this would resolve both pressures in the long term. Similarly, the short-term problem of labour shortages in agriculture meant that the long-term human principle of 'to each according to his or her need' was replaced by 'to each according to his or her work'. How far the long-term goal of developing a non-competitive collective consciousness has been affected by this change of philosophy and the preoccupation with sectoral efficiency in food production is not clear. There is, finally, the short-term goal of increasing productivity via industrialization/technological agriculture versus the long-term requirement of environmental understanding. For Cuba these were, and remain, real dilemmas.

Cuba's food policy dilemmas do not end there. Since the government controls what goes on the market its emphasis on hi-tech agriculture and sugar production has important implications for the Cuban diet. For example, irrigated rice land may be sacrificed to cultivate sugar. This can mean that there is less rice on the ration markets or that it is more expensive on the parallel markets. Root crops, for example, are in short supply because unlike sugar they do not earn foreign exchange. Their production is also given low priority by the government because they have a prolonged growing season, requiring a great deal of hand labour. This does not fit easily with the government's mechanization programme. Meat production, on the other hand, is given high priority. This is because the government seems to see the Western diet as best. It appears to represent a model by which development is gauged. However, if we are to take a wider view of development we should include a critical assessment of the Western diet.

Should underdeveloped countries, like Cuba which has achieved 'basic needs' development through socialism, follow the food policy model of industrialized countries? With respect to hi-tech agriculture I have suggested that this is not necessarily desirable. Though technology has a very important role to play in development strategies, socialism does not imply a technological imperative. Even with non-capitalist governments, cultural and ecological dimensions should be seen as interactive with, rather than prescribed by, modernization.

Hi-tech agriculture is not the only approach Cuba has imported from the West. The same is true of food processing. Once again this is related to the government's view that the Western diet is superior.

What about the ecological consequences of food processing? While indirect food additives such as pesticides and agrochemicals have received considerable attention in debates about development and ecology, direct food additives used in processing tend to have been neglected. Cuba is no exception. The government there does not seem to have developed comprehensive policies towards malnutrition in its overconsumptive forms. Ironically, to appreciate the policy issues which arise we have to start with the West's attempts to control highly industrialized (and by this token often thought of as highly 'developed') food processing.

Social Choice and the Politics of Food Additives

I have already commented on how plant breeding technologies are likely to affect our choice of food systems. I would now like to outline some of the social choices that need to be made in the West with respect to food processing. For brevity, I shall confine the discussion to the control of food additives in the United Kingdom (UK) and the United States of America (US). This does not mean, however, that the issues are irrelevant to Third World development. Quite the contrary is the case.

The global impact of the food processing industry means that, although most of the food processing techniques and accompanying additives originate in the West, both the techniques and the products can be exported to the Third World. Chetley (1986) explains very well how food processing is crucial to the increased profits of the transnational companies involved in the production and marketing of milk products in Third World countries.

The basic idea is that milk is bought up by manufacturers as a raw material and then transformed or 'processed' into milk derivatives such as cheeses, yoghurts, milk-based cereals etc. These are promoted as, and seen as, more desirable luxury food items and hence can be sold to sufficiently wealthy consumers at much higher prices than the manufacturers paid for the raw materials. The products then have 'added value' to the food industry.

The reason why most processing originates in the West is that this is where the most industrialized countries are to be found. The 'industrial revolution' has meant growing urbanization in the West and most importantly, large centres of relatively wealthy consumers who can afford to buy processed foods. Hence marketing processed foods tends to be easier in the West. Due to the poverty of most of the people in the Third World intense marketing of processed foods is required so it is a less attractive market to transnational companies.

On the other hand, Third World governments generally have less developed and stringent political control on food pricing for processed foods than in the West. This factor can make Third World markets particularly favourable and in particular can result in the expansion of large companies into Latin America aiming to sell processed products which have outgrown their demand in the West. It follows that decisions taken about the nutritional and health acceptability of processed foods in the Western diet imply at least a first approximation of their acceptability for sale in the Third World and hence can inform our judgements of marketing claims.

For non-capitalist countries like Cuba, the same principle about health and nutrition applies, even though the 'value added' by the indigenous food processing industry is controlled by the government and distributed by egalitarian mechanisms.

Having crash-coursed the relevance to the Third World of health and nutrition controversies in the West, let us look at what some of those controversies are and where food additives fit in. The potato crisp is as good a place as any to start.

In 1985 British consumers were expected to buy another 3·8 billion packets of crisps at a cost of £467 million. As with milk products when we buy a standard packet of crisps a great deal has been added on to the price. In fact, as Millstone (1986) points out, we would be buying one penny's worth of potato solids which have been processed into a cooked, preserved, flavoured, packaged, advertised, and delivered product of 12p. The point is that food additives are crucial to this 'value adding' activity. Flavourings can create the sense that bacon or prawns have contributed to the final flavour of the crisps. Antioxidants guard against the oil in the crisps going rancid and so on.

The problem with this process from the consumer's point of view is that there is growing evidence to suggest that some of these additives may be toxic and, further, there is little or no evidence to suggest that most of them are demonstrably safe. It is because of the potential toxicity of food additives and their widespread consumption that governments have set up regulatory authorities to control the food industry's sale of them.

Historically, governments have banned the sale of certain additives because they have considered them to be unsafe for human consumption. Cyclamate, a non-nutritive artificial sweetener was banned from use in foods by both the US and the UK regulatory authorities in 1969 after experimentation suggested it might be carcinogenic. Amaranth, a red colouring was banned in the US in several stages during the 1970s due to its teratological effects in rats (Verrett and Carper, 1974). Many question marks hang over the safety of additives currently permitted in the US and the UK.

For example, nitrites in meat products such as bacon are known to form potent carcinogenic substances (nitrosamines) when mixed with amines in the medium of gastric juices. Also saccharin, an artificial sweetener, has been linked to bladder cancer in rats (Priebe and Kaufmann, 1980). Indeed in 1982 the American National Research Council (NRC) was able to report that 21 food additives were suspected or proven to be carcinogenic to laboratory animals (Committee on Diet, Nutrition and Cancer, Assembly of Life Sciences, NRC, 1982).

But those who represent and speak for the industry argue that we need additives. At least two claims of this nature are made. First, that if we are to live in an industrial society with a 'modern food industry' then food additives are a technological necessity (Weedon, 1976). And secondly, that modern food technology has brought an increased variety in food products offering consumers a diet which is convenient, cheap, attractively presented and adequately balanced between fresh and processed food (Marsh, 1983; Stocker, 1983).

The underlying assumption is that food processing has brought social progress and that the industry's development of processed foods is purely a response to consumer demand. Overall, we are given the impression that the toxic effects of food additives are either irrelevant or trivial by comparison to the social benefits.

Notice, that within this argument there is no mention of the nutritional value of additives. This is because, by definition, food additives are not added to food for nutritional purposes (Ministry of Agriculture, Fisheries and Food (MAFF), 1976a). This does not mean that no additives are of nutritional value – just that it will be incidental to the reason the food manufacturers have for using them.

The first thing to realize is that all additives cannot be assessed in a blanket way. Ascorbic acid ie vitamin C is a food additive. Similarly, food processing *per se* is not undesirable. The wholemeal loaf is, for example, a product of food processing and it is cheap and nutritious for consumers. Nevertheless, when the food industry claims it is responding to consumer demand we are entitled to ask how consumers can be demanding chemicals they know little or nothing about. Do consumers know that about 80 per cent of all additives are non-nutritional? (MAFF, 1976b). Do consumers know the risks attached to consuming certain additives? The answer to these questions is almost certainly 'No'. There are two reasons for this.

First, toxicology is characterized by a great deal of uncertainty. Different regulatory authorities come to different decisions about the same food additive. For example, Amaranth is banned in the US but permitted in the UK. Different scientific institutions which test food additives produce vastly different toxicity evaluation data on the same additive. One authoritative report of toxicity testing carried out by the National Academy of Sciences (NAS) suggests that the expected number of cases of human bladder cancer in the US resulting from daily exposure of 120mg of saccharin might range from 0·22 to 1,144,000. (Wilkinson, 1983, cf Silverglade, 1983). In addition to these uncertainties regulatory policy usually has to extrapolate animal toxicity data to a likely toxic effect in humans. Hence without scrutinizing toxicological controversies consumers cannot know the true risks involved. If they did consumer 'demand', as the food industry calls it, might well be altered.

Secondly, it is difficult for consumers to obtain information about the risks of additives. In Britain the members of the Food Advisory Committee (FAC) and its scientific subcommittees are caught by the Official Secrets Act. This means that consumers cannot demand access to the data on which British regulatory decisions are made but rather, they must rely on the discretion of the government to pass on information when and how it wishes. This is disturbing since the British government does not systematically regulate flavourings which probably make up around 3,500 of the total 3,800 additives used in Britain.

In the US the situation is not so secret since consumers have access to the Freedom of Information Act. However, even this act has a trade secrecy exemption clause which probably means that consumers are only able to demand access to safety evaluation data generated by government testing establishments like the Food and Drug Administration (FDA) but not data generated by privately controlled laboratories.

We can see that if consumers are to have a real choice they need to be critically informed and able to participate in the decision-making process. This would entail the relevant regulatory authorities affording delegatory representation to consumers and consumer groups on their committees. Also toxicological experts should certainly be asked to clarify technical problems and controversies but there is no good reason why they should have special powers in making policy decisions. Their role would be to demystify, in the service of a democratically discussed decision-making process.

Finally, when there is a dispute among different experts, as is often the case in this field of 'science', the benefit of the doubt should be given to consumers. In other words if there is evidence that an additive is unacceptably toxic but also evidence disputing this toxicity and no clear way of discounting either claim then the chemical should be considered too toxic to add to food. On the whole, current policies in the US and the UK seem to embrace the opposite approach – 'safe until proven toxic'. In the case of flavourings this might mean waiting many decades until a whole battery of toxicological tests are completed. By that time we will already be suffering any chronic toxicity which these tests might uncover. In the meantime we are engaged in a sort of epidemiological experiment called eating.

Human Development and the Educational Context

It is difficult, if not impossible, to see how the enterprise of capitalism can sensibly tackle the central problems of food and development. We have seen how profit motivated and environmentally shortsighted corporate control of food production exaggerates the long-term problems of the poor and hungry. Further, it is difficult to see how competitive agrosystems in the Third World can lead to development for the poor because they start the race at such a cruel disadvantage. We have seen how the introduction of new agricultural technologies in such competitive situations tends to aggravate inequalities and has little to do with feeding the hungry. I think we have seen that human development has to be based on non-competitive social relations which are collective and encourage sharing of the world's resources.

At the same time we have seen how a more egalitarian society such as Cuba is able to feed all its people despite massive international pressures pushing against the 'basic needs first' policy. Yet even here, emphasis on the Western model of agriculture and diet means that important discussions about the future of food production and the environment can be swept aside. I think this shows us that human development also has to have room for imagination and criticism. Governments must be open to, and encourage, criticism by creating decentralized decision-making bodies which can take account of indigenous culture and environmental understanding.

Finally, we have seen that real social choices in food policy even when 'basic needs' are fully met still need to be made and they require knowledge, understanding and democracy. Human development requires that people are informed so that they can knowingly participate in decisions and choices.

I will call this programme for human development 'socialist'. It is strange that education systems rarely engage with socialist principles. It is strange because we might be forgiven for thinking that the ideals of sharing, collective work, non-competitiveness, criticism, knowledge, understanding and democracy are all principles upon which education ought to be based.

The implication is surely that shifting our world in the direction of human development will itself involve, and depend upon, the development of a socialist education.

References

Bardhan, K. and P. (1973) The green revolution and socioeconomic tensions: the case of India. In *International Social Science Journal* **XXV** (3), pp. 285-292.

Barney, G. (1980) *The Global 2000 Report to the President*. Penguin, Harmondsworth.

Benjamin, M. *et al* (1984) *No Free Lunch: Food and Revolution in Cuba Today*. Institute for Food and Development Policy, San Francisco.

Brown, L. (1975) *By Bread Alone*. Pergamon Press Overseas Development Council, Oxford.

Bull, D. (1982) *A Growing Problem: Pesticides and the Third World*. Oxfam (ch 5).

Cherfas, J. 'Contraceptive inflation'. In *New Scientist* 17 May 1979, p. 527.

Chetley, A. (1986) *The Politics of Baby Foods: Successful Challenges to an International Marketing Strategy*. Frances Pinter, London.

Clutterbuck, C. and Lang, T. (1982) *More Than We Can Chew*. Pluto Press (Ch.2).

Collins, J. *et al* (1982) *What Difference Could a Revolution Make?* Institute for Food and Development Policy, San Francisco.

Food and Agriculture Association (FAO) (1977). *The Fourth World Food Survey*. Food and nutrition series **10** pp. 47-55.

FAO (1985) *Fifth World Food Survey*.

FAO (1986) FAO in 1985. In *World Food Report 1986*. p.29.

Floyd, B. Socialist transformation of agriculture in the Caribbean. Paper presented at the 1978 Annual Conference, Society for Caribbean Studies.

George, S. (1976) *How the other Half Dies*. Pelican Books.

Griffin, K.B. (1974) *The Political Economy of Agrarian Change*. Macmillan, London and Basingstoke.

Grigg, D. (1985) *The World Food Problem 1950–1980*. Basil Blackwell, Oxford.

Hartmann, B. and Standing, H. (1985) *Food, Saris and Sterilisation*. Bangladesh International Action Group, London.

Hilsum, L. (1987) 'Food production improves in Africa'. In *The Guardian*, 3 January, p.7.

Lappe, J.M. and Collins, J. (1982) *Food First*. Abacus.

Ledbetter, R. (1984) Thirty years of family planning in India: In *Asian Survey* **XXIV** (7) July, pp. 736-758.

Leogrande, W.M. (1978) *Cuban Dependency*. Council On International Studies.

Magdoff, F. (1980) Impressions of Cuban agriculture. In *Monthly Review*, June, pp. 35-40.

Malthus, T.R. (1798) *An Essay on the Principle of Population*. Reprinted, (1906) Macmillan, London.

Mamdani, M. (1972) *The Myth of Population Control*. Monthly Review Press, New York.

Mars, Z. (ed.) (1978) The 'green revolution' and rural technology development. In *Research Digest* 2, Autumn. Institute Development Studies, University of Sussex.

Marsh, J. (1983) The food industry in the public interest. In J. Burns *et al* (eds.) *The Food Industry* Heinemann and Commonwealth Bureaux.

Marshall, A. (1984) Africa faces up to overpopulation. In *New Scientist* 2 February, pp. 10-11.

Meadows, D. and D. (1972) *The Limits To Growth* Earth Island, London.

Millstone, E. (1986) *Food Additives: Taking the Lid Off What We Really Eat*, Ch 1, Penguin Books.

Ministry of Agriculture, Fisheries and Foods (MAFF) (1976a) *Food, Quality and Safety: a Century of Progress*. Her Majesty's Stationery Office (HMSO).

MAFF (1976b) *Manual of Nutrition* HMSO.

Mosher, S.W. (1982) Birth control: a view from a Chinese village. In *Asian Survey* **XXIII** (4) April, pp. 356-368.

National Research Council (NRC) (1982) *Diet, Nutrition and Cancer*. National Academy Press.

New Internationalist (1987) Counting the Hungry. February, p.26.

North, R. (1986) *The Real Cost*. Chatto and Windus, London.

Pearce, F. (1984a) The threat of overpopulation wanes. In *New Scientist* 16 August p.8.

Pearce, F. (1984b) In defence of population growth. In *New Scientist* 9 August.

Plumwood, V. and Routley, R. (1981-82) World rainforest destruction – the social factors. In *Ecologist* vol **11/12** pp. 4-22.

Prahladachar, M. (1983) Income distribution effects of the green revolution in India: a review of empirical evidence. In *World Development* 11 (11) pp. 927-944.

Priebe, P.M. and Kaufman, G.B. (1980) Controversy about Saccharin. In *Minerva* pp. 556-574.

Reutlinger, S. and Alderman, H. (1980) The prevalence of calorie deficient diets in developing countries. In *World Development* 8 pp. 399-411.

Reutlinger, S. and Selowsky, M. (1976) Malnutrition and poverty. Magnitude and policy options. World Bank Staff Occasional Papers No.23 pp. 8-38.

Silverglade, B.A. (1983) The risks of risk assessment and risk-benefit analysis. In *Food, Drug and Cosmetic Law Journal* 38 p.31.

Stocker, T. (1983) Pressures on Policy Formation. In J. Burns *et al* (eds.) *The Food Industry* Heinemann and Commonwealth Bureaux.

Tabah, L. (1975) The significance of the Bucharest conference on population. In *International Social Science Journal* XXVII (2), pp. 375-384.

Tudge, C. (1979) *The Famine Business*. Penguin.

Verrett, J. and Carper, J. (1974) *Eating May Be Hazardous to your Health*. Anchor Press, New York.

Vines, G. (1985) Bangladeshis coerced into sterilisation. In *New Scientist* 19 September, pp. 20-21.

Weedon, B.C.L. (1976) Advising on food standards in the UK. In (MAFF) *Food, Quality and Safety: a century of progress* HMSO.

Wilkinson, C. (1983) *Proceedings of 10th International Congress on Plant Protection 1983* Vol 1 p.46, quoted in *Chemistry and Industry* 17 December 1984, p.864.

Yoxen, (1983) *The Gene Business*, Pan Books, London.

Chapter 1.3

THE BASIS OF A RADICAL CURRICULUM IN ENVIRONMENTAL EDUCATION

David Pepper,
Oxford Polytechnic

Radical Environmentalism

It would be difficult to overestimate the magnitude of the social, economic and cultural changes which are implicitly or explicitly demanded by radical environmentalists. Whether you are a 'blue-, 'green- or 'red-green', if you think through the implications of your green position you will probably conclude that the prerequisite for establishing your kind of caring, ecologically harmonious society is that the roots of the existing society should be hacked away. Most of the seminal polemical works of ecocentric literature (O'Riordan, 1981) of the past 15 years make this much, at least, clear (Goldsmith *et al*, 1972; Schumacher, 1973; Skolimowski, 1981; Porritt, 1984). They also frequently suggest that education will play a major role in achieving the radical changes they want. However, since education is currently more a means of maintaining the political and economic *status quo* than anything else, then nothing short of radical reform of the curriculum, and the system, is demanded. Of course, what curricular reforms you demand will substantially depend on where with in the spectrum of green politics you lie.

If you are 'blue-green' you will probably yearn for the re-establishment of what you take to be a 'natural' order of society, where people were hierarchically organized (and apparently content about it) and in an 'organic' and partly metaphysical relationship to nature. Such an order, you may decide on peering through your rose-coloured romantic lenses, existed in 'pre-industrial' societies. This of course is a very old conservative outlook, though it may be dressed up in modern 'systems' jargon (Goldsmith, 1978). It holds that nature and the natural order set limits to human aspirations, which, therefore, must acknowledge the primacy of biological laws like that of carrying capacity (Hardin, 1968, 1974). It tries to preserve what is left of natural resources (Meadows *et al*, 1972) or 'traditional' landscapes (Shoard, 1980) without asking too many questions about whom they are to be preserved for. Hence, 'blue-green' educational priorities tend to stem from the laws of ecology, and to work from these to the social world.

By contrast, 'red-greens' emphasize how nature and natural things are substantially social constructs, contingent on world views and social relationships that cannot be fully appreciated in isolation from the material economic organization of society. (Schnaiberg, 1980; Sandbach, 1980; Smith and O'Keefe, 1980). The corollary of this is that progressive ecological change is to be achieved only in a dialectical relationship with social change and corresponding changes in material economic organization. In concrete terms this means changes of the kind envisaged by anarcho-socialists (Ward, 1986; Bookchin, 1980). The educational priorities are therefore social, and ecological reform is seen as contingent on social reform.

Like others in the middle ground of politics, if you are a 'green-green' your position may represent an amalgam of notions and practices drawn from both left and right (Capra and Spretnak, 1984; Porritt, 1984) – while often claiming that you are aloof from both and represent something politically 'new' (Capra, 1982). Your ideal world is summed up in Callenbach's *Ecotopia* (1975, 1981), where biology dominates the school curriculum but social morality and alternative economic organization also dominate the socialization process.

As I have argued elsewhere (Pepper, 1984, 1985, 1986A) my preferred position is that of the 'red-greens'. In what follows I am, therefore, adopting a set of curricular aims which are most compatible with this position. (Also, I argue essentially from the perspective of higher education.) I believe, of course, that the fulfilment of these aims is a minimal requirement if education is to play anything like the role which is often claimed for it as the cutting edge of radical social and ecological change. And, of course, it remains an open question as to whether education can fulfil this role at all.

The Aims of the Curriculum

1. To criticize conventional wisdoms

The first aim of a radical curriculum in environmental education must be to challenge and undermine the conventional wisdoms of our society, which has a world view substantially predicated on the assumption of capitalist ideology. These wisdoms function to legitimate, strengthen and reproduce that ideology, along with the system of capitalism itself. Since classical science is a major component of this world view, (Merchant, 1982) the assumptions of scientific epistemology must be brought to the surface and questioned. Furthermore, to the extent that environmentalism *itself* serves to reinforce rather than undermine the socio-political *status quo* (Papadakis, 1984; Ensensberger, 1974) *its* assumptions and aims should also be analysed.

2. To explore the material and ideological bases of conventional wisdoms

In achieving this first aim, we must avoid the strategy of attempting to assess the 'rightness' or 'wrongness' of the components of our world view or our beliefs about nature, against some supposed rational or objective criteria. This would lead immediately to acceptance of the primacy of rationality and objectivity as against other values. Instead, we should make it our second aim to demonstrate the relationship between people's ideas and values and their material position in society, and between dominant social ideologies and economic organization. In other words, we should attempt, through a materialist, historical analysis, to see where ideas and values come from, and why some are given social pre-eminence as against others (Russell, 1946).

3. To open students' minds to alternative world views

If these two aims have been successfully accomplished, then a third may also have been accomplished – students' minds may have been opened to the existence, validity and viability of 'alternative' world views. Those views which are based on holistic, spiritual, bioethical and socialist values are particularly signifi-cant for radical left environmentalists.

4. To work and live cooperatively

However, a materialist stance must militate against our dwelling overmuch in the realm of ideas. Thus, a fourth major curricular aim must be for students to learn to *work and live cooperatively* rather than competitively, so that the importance and credibility of cooperation as the basis of social organization and ecological harmony can be established.

5. To realize that humans can act collectively to shape society

Finally, neither the third or fourth aims will lead to any lasting outcome unless students can also be weaned away from the most pervasive, insidious and odious educational doctrine of our time – that they are basically powerless in the face of deterministic forces of nature, economics, history and other 'external' influences, to bring about an ecologically sound and socially just society. The fifth, and most important, educational aim, therefore, should be to bring on the realization that humans *can* act collectively and successfully to change and shape their society, and their own nature, to suit themselves.

Curricular Content: The Issues with which Environmental Education Must Connect

The environmental movement

In achieving the first and second curricular aims – to criticize conventional wisdoms and explore their material and ideological bases – it is often effective to consider the environmental movement itself. So many environmental education courses tend to assume that:

1. our prime concerns must be about nature and what humans are doing to it (eg wilderness, wild life and countryside);
2. there *is* an underlying population/resources/pollution crisis;
3. environmental campaigning is invariably a 'good thing' because it challenges us all to put our hearts and minds in order and to stop living ecologically-damaging lifestyles.

Such a challenge is thought to transcend the old political 'squabbles' because nothing less than the future of all humanity is at issue.

The scientific basis of such arguments should first be examined, and the laws and concepts of ecology and related natural sciences should be mastered. Such principles as the carrying capacity, stability-in-diversity, feedback and homeostatis, which underpin many ecocentric social messages, must be understood before the messages can be critically assessed, as must Darwinian concepts like evolution and the web of life. The nature of past and present human impact on natural ecosystems should be studied, along with the supposed natural constraints on population and economic growth which biologists like Hardin, Ehrlich (1970) and Myers (1980) perceive.

From this platform, questions can then be asked about just how much of our environment really is 'natural' – where this implies absence of human influence. In fact, no terrestrial ecosystems at all could be so defined, while very many have been actively *fashioned* by humans. There are no 'natural' ecosystems: most wildernesses or 'traditional' rural landscapes, like our urban landscapes, are the product of human action. Therefore, fights to preserve, for example, Halvergate Marshes or Exmoor are really struggles to preserve those economic activities which produce moor and marsh.

This realization might trigger questions about whether such struggles are the most important ones if we are to improve the environments of most people. For the majority of people, living in poverty, dirt and overcrowding in Western inner cities or Third World shanties or peasant farms on marginal land, the green politics of 'hedgerow, butterfly and bunny-rabbit protection' are an irrelevance (Weston, 1986). *Environmental* issues that concern the mass of people are poverty, malnutrition, poor housing, economic inequality, violence, alienating labour, unemployment, loss of community, and so on. And, inasmuch as they distract attention from these really burning matters and their prime causes in capitalist economic and social arrangements, organizations like Greenpeace or the Council for the Protection of Rural England are merely expressions of middle-class false consciousness. Like Band Aid and Sport Aid's efforts to address Ethiopian environmental problems, they could be regarded as counterproductive. For they make their supporters believe that they have done something fundamental to alleviate the problems, which they do not realize that they have helped to bring about. Hence, through eased consciences and dulled consciousness, real causes continue to go unperceived and unchecked.

The Ethiopian famine is an excellent illustration of how so-called population/resource 'crises' can be invoked to cover a multitude of sins that really originate in the nature of political and economic organization rather than in Malthusian laws. Both right- and left-wing critiques on this major 'environmental' issue are instructive.

Simon (1981) and Simon and Kahn (1984), like Harvey (1974) and Perelman (1979), encourage us to see how resources are not absolute and unchanging but are culturally-defined, as are concepts like 'needs' and 'subsistence'. They stress the importance of production and human ingenuity as valuable forms of resource. Like Chase (1980), they also dwell on the race and class prejudice which often underlies population concern. Common ground ends there, for Harvey and Perelman, following Marx, show how resource depletion and an apparent population surplus will always tend to be generated by *laissez-faire* capitalism, while Simon and Kahn argue that this system alone can cope with 'overpopulation' and scarcity through the market, by encouraging thrift, substitution, and universal affluence.

Both critiques are indispensable in exposing the considerable shortcomings of reports like *Limits to Growth* (Meadows *et al*, 1972) and *Global 2000* (Barney, 1980). They also show that environmental questions are deeply political in traditional left-right terms, and claims that they are 'above' the 'old' politics (Ecology Party, 1979, 1983) do not withstand close scrutiny. Such a scrutiny should be applied, leading on to an analysis of the political spectrum of greens in terms of basic conservative, liberal and socialist ideologies. The awareness that this fosters should stand in marked contrast to the political naivety of very many green supporters.

Attitudes to nature
The history of Western attitudes and attitude changes should be studied. To go back to study the medieval cosmology, whose geocentric universe and 'great chain of being's' organizing principles were physico-theological, is not simply fascinating. It also leads to two rather unsettling realizations. First, that this 'peculiar' cosmology constituted as logical a perspective on nature and the environment as our own, and, second, that elements of the cosmology may have persisted strongly into recent and even current environmental beliefs. Glacken (1967), Thomas (1983), Worster (1985), Oldroyd (1980), Capra (1982) and Merchant (1982) all bring this out when they help us to trace the development of the world view of classical science, and its application to the animal and human worlds via Malthus, Darwin, Huxley, Herbert Spencer and the like.

Such an exercise in historical imagination profoundly disturbs our mental complacency, making us realize how recent are ideas and perceptions which we had held to be eternal and natural verities, or 'common sense'. Empiricism, reductionism, the primacy of analytical and rational thought, objectivity (in the Cartesian sense) and the idea of the world as a machine – all these concepts have permeated and informed mass consciousness for only the past three hundred years or less. To learn this, and, therefore, that the conceptual foundations of our 'developed' society are not historically deep, may bring us up with a jerk. Many ecocentrics have learnt this, and they want to tilt the balance of prevailing ideologies more in favour of the 'medieval' values of holism and synthesis, and intuitive, spiritual and emotionally-founded knowledge of nature, which they see as an organism (Sagan and Margalis, 1983; Freer, 1983; Hughes, 1982).

However, the history of our developing relationship with nature is not primarily a story of ideas, and White (1967) oversimplifies when he says that what we do about ecology depends on our *ideas* about nature. Thomas (1983) is nearer the mark when he draws out the correspondence between what people *do* to nature and what ideas they hold about it in legitimation of their action. Therefore, the evolution of modern industrial capitalism and of European industrial society, and how they advanced across the globe in only two or three hundred years must be studied in order that this correspondence between ideas and action may be perceived. The relevance of ideologies about nature – like social Darwinism, scientific materialism, the Baconian creed and faith in technology – to capitalist productive relationships needs to be seen so that the true magnitude of environmentalist prescriptions involving wholesale value changes can be appreciated.

Philosophy
If, through studying modern industrial capitalist society students begin to see where their world views came from, then the third curricular objective – of opening their minds to *alternative* world views – should become more realizable. However, this process of shaking entrenched beliefs concerning the certainty, inevitability and exclusive 'correctness' of the elements making up our own cultural ideological filter is not an easy one. One route that may be followed to establish that intellectual uncertainty, which is the prerequisite for an open weighing-up of unfamiliar 'new' ideas, goes from historical to philosophical study.

Two of the most important questions which environmentalists ask are, first, whether humans are separate from nature, and, second, whether we in the West can continue to behave as if there are no natural limits to human achievement. Underlying these questions is the old philosophical opposition of determinism and free will.

Some sort of determinism – environmental, biological, economic, cultural, historical or religious – is part of the intellectual baggage of most Westerners, and is an essential component of classical science. It suggests one-way cause/effect relationships between humans and nature. It also may imply that our power to shape our society as we wish is circumscribed by natural laws – indeed the very nature of society and the individuals that comprise it may be seen as substantially shaped by 'external' forces.

The opposing free-will philosophies, like existentialism and phenomenology, can open up minds to very different implications, but not without difficulty, since their neglect has been so comprehensive that even the language to convey their concepts barely exists. These implications are that there *are* no externally-produced natural (or social) laws by which individuals must be bound, beyond the one certainty of eventual death. Hence we may *choose* how we will live, and treat nature and each other. Such freedom means that we, and no-one else, bear entire responsibility for our actions towards nature, be they exploitative or caring. Moreover, the very validity of conceiving nature, as separate from, and external to human consciousness is challenged. In this view, not only are Descartes' 'secondary' qualities (colour, smell, taste) subjective products of the mind: the supposedly fixed and objective 'primary' qualities (position, size, shape, momentum) of nature are in reality similarly produced. We thus fashion nature from our minds, and we can, therefore, make of it what we wish. The answer to that old philosophical conundrum of whether a tree continues to exist when we turn our back on it is 'no'. There can be no 'nature' without human consciousness to create and interpret it, and therefore it is pointless to divorce the study of the two.

Clearly, such mind-stretching concepts, which also admit mystical knowledge of the universe (eg, Bach, 1978) will be alien to the perceptions of students from many backgrounds. As such, they are likely to be received with suspicion as well as incredulity. But such is the legitimating power of science, however, that if very similar ideas are introduced via 'post-classical' science – ie subatomic physics (Capra, 1975; Zukav, 1980) – they may be received with more respect and consideration. The wave-particle and position-momentum paradoxes, for example, relativity theory, and the dynamic picture of the universe as a constant transmutation of energy and matter – all of these concepts are valuable weapons in the fight against unquestioning determinism among the young. They confirm that there is, at least at the level of fundamental particles, no external nature, made of 'solid' building blocks like atoms, to determine us. The logical implication is that 'laws' of nature are, in theory if not in practice, merely mental organizing concepts by which we have tried to create order out of seeming chaos. Such ideas, together with free-will philosophies, Eastern mysticism and Western transcendentalism should form an essential part of the environmental curriculum's antidote to the strait jacket of scientific materialism. They may, at the least, stimulate interest in unfamiliar epistemologies, cultures and lifestyles, so that essential facets of ecocentric philosophy and sub-culture – approached, for example, through meditation and involving Buddhism or paganism – will not be rejected out of hand.

The political message

A further and most pertinent reason for weaning students away from purely deterministic beliefs lies in the fulfilment of the fifth curricular aim, concerned with political action to achieve social change. Neo-Malthusian and social Darwinist arguments, where 'nature' is used to legitimate the political, economic and social *status quo*, are rife today (especially in the neo-conservatism which prevails in the US and UK). They are deterministic because they hold that certain prevailing states of affairs or social behaviours are 'natural', and, since this is so, they are therefore acceptable and inevitable. To try to counter them merely goes against nature, and is futile.

To challenge the credibility of such fatalistic, do-nothing doctrines, it is worth studying their history. A remarkable fact comes to light, which is that the so-called 'natural order' discerned by biologists like Darwin, Huxley, Tansley and Clements, was in reality quite clearly and explicitly *first* transferred by analogy *from* society *to* nature, before being transferred *back* from nature to society in social Darwinism or social ecology. Thus, as Engels noted, the principles of competition, struggle for existence and survival of the fittest were taken from Hobbes' and Malthus' observations of capitalist society and imposed, in Darwinian evolution, on to plant and animal behaviour patterns (Oldroyd, 1980). Similarly, the concepts of plant succession and climax in the colonization of new areas were taken by analogy from the sequence of human settlement in the American West. (Then this supposed 'natural' order of plant succession, from simple to complex, was used in subsequent political legitimation of particular land uses. (Worster, 1985).

Whereas, social Darwinism and Malthusianism are forms of *environmental* determinism, where nature's resource limits substantially shape social behaviour (Huxley, 1888); *biological* determinism internalizes social behaviour as the product of the inherited characteristics of the individuals who make up society. Thus, the nature of 'human nature' is a crucial matter for environmentalists because so many socialist and green utopias are predicated on the idea that people *can* and will behave in less selfish and individualistic ways than they do under capitalism. If, however, behaviour were principally inherited, and if what was transmitted in our genes was essentially greedy and selfish (Dawkins, 1976) – as so many British middle-class students seem firmly to believe – then all the utopias will ultimately flounder, and socialist-green politics are doomed to failure. The biological studies by Stephen Gould and Steven Rose can be invoked here. Rose,

Kamin and Lewontin (1984), for example, systematically and relentlessly demolish biological determinism, and expose its tendency to explain partly social phenomena – like IQ, and sex differences – solely in biological terms, for the political ideology which it is.

And we can turn to Kropotkin's (1902) ecological studies to see that it is feasible to read social messages from nature that are diametrically opposed to those which social Darwinists derive in order to legitimate capitalism. His conclusion that:

'In the ethical progress of man, mutual support – not mutual struggle – has had the leading part. In its wide extension, even at the present time, we also see the best guarantee of a still loftier evolution of our race.'

is echoed strongly by Capra (1982), and it confirms the essentially socialist-anarchist basis of radical and progressive green thought (Bookchin, 1980).

Kropotkin (Ward, 1986) also provided the vision of an alternative society, based on small-scale, decentralist, energy-conserving and anti-capitalist economic principles, which has been echoed strongly three-quarters of a century later in the *Blueprint for Survival* (Goldsmith *et al*, 1972) and *Ecotopia* (Callenbach, 1975). Such utopias, along with many others in Western thought (Manuel and Manuel, 1979), and attempts to establish them in practice (Hardy, 1979) ought to be closely studied. They drive home the essential connection between achieving socio-economic change and ecological harmony.

Doing It

To lead students, thus, to appreciate the primacy of social justice as the prerequisite of ecological harmony, is one essential component of the radical environmental curriculum. To help the theoretical understanding of how such social change comes about is another. But if we accept the point of Marxist materialist analysis we cannot leave it there, imagining that social change is attainable merely via the abstract study of ideas and through appeals for people to change, through education, their values. Meaningful change can only come about through the concurrent development of theory and *practice*. It is this proposition which presents the greatest challenge for the radical environmental educator. How can students be helped to *live and work* in cooperative ways in a capitalistic competitive environment, to hold other people and nature in equal regard with themselves, and to learn non-violent, non-materialist and non-exploitative behaviours?

One can envisage a scale of progressively more radical teaching approaches and concomitant activities. The further one goes along this scale, towards active rather than passive learning and towards education via hand and brain, the more likely it is that the lives of students will be permanently affected by their educational experiences.

At the relatively conventional end of the scale, students would be required and encouraged to work in groups on joint projects, jointly assessed, which would largely replace the more familiar individualistic examination. They would be led towards active participative learning through group research and presentations in topics largely of their choosing, and by being asked to assess their own work. The teacher would facilitate learning but not instruct – giving advice on curriculum content, literary and other source material, and also on how to approach group work so that each member plays a valued and valuable role.

Along with such learning approaches, first-hand knowledge of people who are actually attempting to forge social and environmental change must be sought. Students might visit workers in environmental management or in the design, production and use of alternative technology (such as 'soft' energy or organic farming). Or they may visit more radical groups, who are trying to create viable alternative communities such as self-sustaining communes and/or housing and producer cooperatives. They may also talk to environmental pressure group campaigners to learn about the issues which concern them and how they go about influencing opinions and policies.

Much further along the scale will be courses that require students to *participate* in the life and work of alternative communities or campaigning groups. The effectiveness of such involvement is likely to increase with time. Whereas a week's 'field course' might bring largely cerebral benefits, a six-month or one-yearly commitment, as in an industrial or professional placement, would make a far more indelible mark.

And, finally, at the 'extreme' end of the scale one can envisage cooperatively-run free institutions where students largely design their own curriculum. This curriculum would not be directed only towards the kinds of content discussed above. It would also involve substantial interaction with the local community in activities which aim to create alternative social and economic arrangements there. The institutions that sustain this education would, themselves, ideally be part of a system of mutually interdependent alternative communities and enterprises, dedicated to production and to social life as well as to education goals. The schools and the polytechnic which serve and are served by the Mondragon cooperatives in Spain approximate to this model. Thus, this end of the scale would be firmly based on Thoreau's (1974) anarchistic educational principles:

'Students should not *play* life or *study* it meekly, while the community supports them, but earnestly *live* it from beginning to end.

'Which would have advanced the most at the end of the month – the boy who had made his own jack-knife from the ore which he had dug or smelted, reading as much as would be necessary for this – or the boy who had attended the lectures on metallurgy at the institute in the meanwhile, and had received a Rodgers penknife from his father?

'[Instead of collecting money for a college to be built] following blindly the principle of division of labour to its extreme – a principle which should never be followed but with circumspection – and calling in Irish labourers ... It would be better than this, for the students, or those who desire to be benefited by it, even to lay the foundations themselves.

'Tuition ... is an important item in the term bill, while for the far more valuable education which he gets by associating with the most cultivated of his contemporaries, no charge is made.

Conclusions

Two classes of impediment to achieving the content and approaches of the radical environmental curriculum come to mind. First, the most 'extreme' and effective approaches, involving the free institution as an organic part of the local community, is least likely to fit in with the organization, structure and ethos of the conventional higher education system in most, or all, Western countries. The British university, polytechnic or college, for example, is very hierarchical; learning is largely passive and one-way (from tutor to students); the system is competitive and individualistic; the timetable increasingly fragments the learning experience and does not even favour long courses with outside placements unless they are geared to industry. Of course, the curriculum content proposed here is highly interdisciplinary: it might even be denounced by the traditional disciplinary-based academic for displaying the mortal sin of eclecticism. Worse still, it might be thought of as insufficiently 'academic' because of the equality of hand and brain work which it ideally demands.

Secondly, if this kind of environmental curriculum *were* to achieve the aims set out for it above, then it would not be tolerated. It specifically aims to overthrow the *status quo*, whereas most education implicitly or explicitly sustains it. (Hales, 1982; Bowles and Gintis, 1976; Harris, 1979; Huckle, 1985; Pepper, 1983,

1986B). One is, therefore, unlikely to see such a curriculum introduced coherently into the higher education system – only small fragments will find niches.

These fundamental impediments arise because education, contrary to the views of many environmentalists, is not going to be the motor of major social and environmental change (Pepper, 1984). If we want to see the radical curriculum in the radically organized institutions which best suit it, then these institutions have to be part of the larger alternative social and economic system referred to above. Such a system is not likely to be brought about by the efforts of educators and idealists alone. This is why one must remain sceptical about current attempts by environmentalists and radical political intellectuals to establish an alternative university in the Midlands. It is more likely to proceed from the actions of the mass of people, confronted with the increasing inadequacies and contradictions of the capitalist economic system. But precisely how these actions are to come about and how they are to be encouraged must, of course, constitute one of the more important items in the radical environmental curriculum itself.

References

Bach, R. (1978) *Illusions: the Adventures of a Reluctant Messiah*, Pan, London.

Barney, G. (1980) *The Global 2000 Report to the President*. Penguin, Harmondsworth.

Bookchin, M. (1980) *Towards an Ecological Society*, Black Rose Books, Montreal.

Bowles, S. and Gintis, H. (1976) *Schooling in Capitalist America*, Routledge and Kegan Paul, London.

Callenbach, E. (1975) *Ecotopia*. Banyon Tree Books, California.

Callenbach, E. (1981) *Ecotopia Emerging*. Banyon Tree Books, California.

Capra, F. (1975) *The Tao of Physics*, Fontana, London.

Capra, F. (1982) *The Turning Point*, Wildwood House, London.

Capra, F. and Spretnak (1984) *Green Politics: the Global Promise*. Hutchinson, London.

Chase, A. (1980) *The Legacy of Malthus: the Social Costs of the New Scientific Racism*, University of Illinois Press, Urbana.

Dawkins, R. (1976) *The Selfish Gene*, Oxford University Press, Oxford.

Ecology Party (1979) *The Real Alternative*. Election manifesto, The Ecology Party, Birmingham.

Ecology Party (1983) *Politics for Life*. Election manifesto, The Ecology Party, London.

Ehrlich, P. (1970) *The Population Bomb*, Ballantine Books, New York.

Ensensberger, H. (1974) A critique of political ecology. In *New Left Review*, **84**, pp. 3-32.

Freer, J. (1983) Gaia: the Earth, Our Spiritual Heritage. In Caldercott, L. and Lelard, S. (eds.) *Reclaim the Earth*, The Women's Press, London.

Glacken, C. (1967) *Traces on the Rhodian Shore*, University of California Press, Berkeley.

Goldsmith, E. (1978) The religion of a stable society. In *Man-Environment Systems*, **8**, pp. 13-24.

Goldsmith, E., Allan, R., Allaby, M., Davoll, J. and Lawrence, S. (1972) *Blueprint for Survival*, Penguin, Harmondsworth.

Hales, D. (1982) *Science or Society?* Pan Books/Channel 4, London.

Hardin, G. (1968) Tragedy of the Commons. In *Science*, **162**, pp. 1243-1248.

Hardin, G. (1974) Living on a lifeboat. In *Bioscience*, **24**, p.10.

Hardy, D. (1979) *Alternative Communities in Nineteenth-Century England*, Longman, London.

Harris, K. (1979) *Education and Knowledge*, Routledge and Kegan Paul.

Harvey, D. (1974) Population, resources and the ideology of science. In *Economic Geography*, **50**, pp. 256-277.

Huckle, J. (1985) Geography and Schooling. In Johnston, R. (ed.) *The Future of Geography*, Methuen, London.

Hughes, J. (1982) Gaia: an Ancient View of Our Planet. In *Ecologist*, **12** (2 and 3), pp. 54-60.

Huxley, T.H. (1888) The struggle for existence in human society. *In The Nineteenth Century*, February.

Kropotkin, P. (1902) *Mutual Aid: a Factor of Evolution*, Porter Sargent, Boston.

Manuel, F.E. and Manuel, F.P. (1979) *Utopian Thought in the Western World*, Basil Blackwell, Oxford.

Meadows, D., Meadows, D., Randers, J. and Behrens, W. (1972) *The Limits to Growth*. Earth Island, London.

Merchant, C. (1982) *The Death of Nature: Women, Ecology and the Scientific Revolution*. Wildwood House, London.

Myers, N. (1980) *The Sinking Ark*, Pergamon, Oxford.

Oldroyd, D.R. (1980) *Darwinian Impacts*. Open University Press, Milton Keynes.

O'Riordan (1981) *Environmentalism*. Pion, 2nd edition, London.

Papadakis, E. (1984) *The Green Movement in West Germany*. Croom Helm, London.

Pepper, D. (1983) Bringing physical and human geographers together: why is it so difficult. In Canon, T., Forbes, M. and Mackie (eds.) *Society and Nature*, London, Union of Socialist Geographers, pp. 19-31.

Pepper, D. (1984) *Roots of Modern Environmentalism*, Croom Helm, London.

Pepper, D. (1985) Determinism, idealism and the politics of environmentalism. *International Journal of Environmental Studies*, 26, pp. 11-19.

Pepper, D. (1986A) Radical environmentalism and the labour movement. In Weston, J. (ed.) *Red and Green: the New Politics of the Environment*, Pluto Press, London, pp. 115-139.

Pepper, D. (1986B) Why teach physical geography? In *Contemporary Issues in Geography and Education*, 2 (2), pp. 62-71.

Perelman, M. (1979) Marx, Malthus and the concept of natural resource scarcity. In *Antipode*, 11 (2), pp. 80-89.

Porritt, J. (1984) *Seeing Green*, Basil Blackwell, Oxford.

Rose, S., Kamin, L.J. and Lewontin, R.C. (1984) *Not in Our Genes*. Penguin, Harmondsworth.

Russell, B. (1946) *History of Western Philosophy*. George Allen and Unwin, London.

Sagan, C. and Margalis, L. (1983) The Gaian perspective on ecology. In *Ecologist*, 13 (5), pp. 160-167.

Sandbach, F. (1980) *Environment, Ideology and Policy*, Basil Blackwell, Oxford.

Schnaiberg, A. (1980) *The Environment: from Surplus to Scarcity*. Oxford University Press, New York.

Schumacher, E.F. (1973) *Small is Beautiful: Economics as if People Really Mattered*. Abacus, London.

Shoard, M. (1980) *Theft of the Countryside*. Temple Smith, London.

Simon, J. (1981) *The Ultimate Resource*, Martin Robertson, Oxford.

Simon, J. and Kahn, H. (1984) *The Resourceful Earth*. Basil Blackwell, Oxford.

Skolimowski, H. (1981) *Eco-Philosophy*. Marion Boyars, London.

Smith, N. and O'Keefe, P. (1980) Geography, Marx and the concept of nature. In *Antipode*, 12 (2), pp. 30-39.

Thomas, K. (1983) *Man and the Natural World: Changing Attitudes in England, 1500–1800*. Allan Lane, London.

Thoreau, H.D. (1974) *Walden*. Collier Books, New York.

Ward, C. (ed.) (1986) *Fields, Factories and Workshops (Tomorrow)*, by P. Kropotkin, Freedom Press, London.

Weston, J. (ed.) (1986) *Red and Green: the New Politics of the Environment*. Pluto Press, London.

White, L. (1967) The historical roots of our ecologic crisis. In *Science*, 155, pp. 1203-07.

Worster, D. (1985) *Nature's Economy: a History of Ecological Ideas*, Cambridge University Press, Cambridge.

Zukav, G. (1980) *The Dancing Wu-Li Masters*, Fontana, London.

PART TWO

PART TWO

INTRODUCTION TO PART TWO

The four papers in this part of the book take a different perspective on the problems of development and environment. The authors start from the viewpoint of their experience within the educational system. They ask questions about why the system is so resistant to reform and what it is possible to achieve given the present constraints. A number of suggestions and strategies for the future emerge from these papers. It is in the conclusion to the whole book that we bring these together and suggest an overarching strategy for their implementation.

A Radical Education Reform

In his paper, Chapter 2.1 (Towards a General Framework for a New Curriculum and Pedagogy) Lacey takes a look at the issues concerned with a radical reform of education. He finds a system of schooling deeply embedded within capitalism and neglected by socialist thinkers and writers. The functions and ideology of schooling he discovers to be so pervaded by, and absorbed into capitalism, that schooling almost constitutes an indoctrination. Consequently, there are very few viable alternative models for socialist educators to practise. Despite the fact that for the four post war decades, a large section of our social life has been managed by socialized institutions – health, social services, education, nationalized industries, etc, – they have not generated a socialist ideology at the institutional level and have not been enlivened and regenerated by critical debate within the education system. They have ignored each other and become individualized, rigid and weak.

Likewise, the issues of development and environment have been ignored or treated within a framework that isolates and trivializes the major problems emerging from these aspects of social life.[1] Lacey finds that the development of a socialist education as a viable strand within our schools would be an almost essential prerequisite for tackling the issues within development and ecology. An analysis of the reasons why the system is as it is leads him to propose areas for reform and the major elements of a socialist education. The major components of this education, 'critical education' and 'constructive education', he sees as non doctrinaire, analytical and, in the long run, essential to the maintenance of openness and democracy in our society.

Assessment

Andy Hargreaves, Chapter 2.2 (Educational Assessment – a Test for Socialism), begins by examining assessment. Examinations are one of the factors that teachers and educationalists usually put forward as being a reason why schools stay the same. Relevant knowledge is defined by the examination syllabus and individual classroom teachers cannot easily change it. Once the curriculum has been defined and written down, it shapes the minds of generation after generation of school children competing for a 'place in the sun'. In addition, examinations shape the kind of teaching that takes place in the classroom; didactic and 'from the front' teaching methods are believed to result from examination pressures and constitute low risk strategies on the part of teachers. Hargreaves looks at those explanations and shows that they retain much of their relevance in today's rapidly changing scene. In addition, it is important to realize that crowded syllabi and previous teacher experiences may also produce authoritarian, didactic styles of teaching. Examination reform will not be a sufficient cause of change in itself. New forms of examination, which are intended to redress or eliminate some of the worst effects of 'old style' public examinations may simply regress to devices for camouflaging these effects. Graded tests, pupil profiles and records of personal achievement are quickly becoming infused with the needs of employers and hidden devices for securing conformity. It is important to understand some of those mechanisms.

Socialists have for too long dodged the difficult issues embedded in the question of assessment. It is important that they now change their priorities. It should now be possible to postpone and downgrade examinations at 16+ without damaging the process of 'fair' selection. The diagnostic and useful aspects of assessment must be retained and space made for new knowledge and new learning experiences in the secondary school curriculum.

Geoff Whitty, Chapter 2.3 (Integrated Humanities: a Curriculum Context for Ecology and Development Education) accepts the major constraints on educational change, as discussed in the earlier papers, but turns his attention to examining what can be accomplished within the present examining system. He finds that 'integrated humanities' provides a valuable context by which to proceed and that persistence and patience can be rewarded by renewed interest and enthusiasm for the kind of topic and pedagogy advanced in this book. This is not to say that integrated humanities is synonymous with a socialist approach to education, but it does represent a context in which many similar concerns can flourish. For example, the SEG, GCSE syllabus is based on aims which can be summarized as

1. An understanding of human societies.
2. An understanding of the social and cultural context of life in a modern society, with respect to personal futures.
3. An awareness of the meaning and diversity of human values.
4. Social, economic and political literacy.
5. Active and collaborative involvement in the learning process.

Topics range from industrialization and the impact of technology through race, culture and gender inequalities to recreation and conservation and world interdependence. In addition, 30 per cent of the marks are awarded for a personal research study and 40 per cent on course work. This kind of development is an extremely encouraging start in the process of re-orientating an examination system largely based on learning curriculum content in areas far removed from these concerns.

John Huckle, in Chapter 2.4 (Environment and Development Issues in the Classroom) provides us with a second example of this kind of curriculum development. Working within the Global Environmental Education Project, funded by the World Wildlife Fund, he has collaborated in the production of curricula with a more explicitly socialist perspective. 'What We Consume' represents a module in the total project. It consists of ten units which range from 'Nature and society', 'The rise of industrial society and our consumer society' through 'Brazil; the destruction of the tropical forest' and 'Ethiopia; war, famine and desertification' to 'Multi-lateral action on the environment' and 'The environment and democracy'. The ten units described by Huckle are very close to the concerns discussed in this book as a whole. He goes on to describe how topics can be taught by actively involving pupils. The unit represents a radical pedagogy linked to socialist concerns about the environment. This is not to say that pupils are forced into conclusions – they are encouraged to ask questions and make their own judgements. While Huckle's project is more explicitly radical than that described by Whitty we should note that it is also more peripheral to the education system. It is not a syllabus offered by an examination board nor is it the kind of project that will be taken up by a majority of schools. This does not detract from its importance; its success will lie in its ability to reveal the inadequacies of current teaching materials on these issues and the appeal of its experiential activities to teachers. Its development will depend on the dedication and skill of radical teachers who are prepared to move forward in an increasingly hostile educational climate. The contribution of part two of this book is an encouraging development that will generate more energy in the battle to educate young people in the realities of the world they live in.

Note

1. This comment is not intended to belittle the excellent work done by teachers and organizations in the areas of World Studies, Development Education, Environmental Education and Peace Studies. The point made here relates to the place of these initiatives within the total curriculum in schools.

Chapter 2.1

TOWARDS A GENERAL FRAMEWORK FOR A NEW CURRICULUM AND PEDAGOGY: PROGRESS TOWARDS A SOCIALIST EDUCATION

Colin Lacey,
University of Sussex

This chapter consists of three parts: a prologue, a recent but unpublished paper 'Where it has to Go Now If We are Serious about Socialism' and a postscript. The aim of the chapter is to uncover some of the basic issues facing an educational reform that wishes to move the education system so that it confronts problems as fundamental as those contained within the areas of 'development' and 'ecology'. The chapter attempts to move over a very wide field in a short space, from a diagnosis of the major ills to a suggested solution. Therefore, I found it helpful to retain the earlier paper in its entirety. The jump between theoretical generality and detailed solution is thereby given a structural reality which, I hope, allows the reader to change gear.

The Prologue

Any argument which suggests that a socialist education can make a relevant or important contribution to some of the most deep-seated problems facing our society must be proposed cautiously and rigorously. If an accusation of indoctrination or bias can be shown to have just a grain of truth then even socialist institutions will turn their backs in fear of being tarred with the same brush. On the other hand, the success and pervasiveness of the dominant capitalist ideology can be measured by one fact. Government ministers can propose that schools introduce pupils to the idea that 'profit' is an essential and healthy part of our economic system giving it dynamism and direction, without fear of public outcry, while 'Peace Education' and other 'controversial' topics are constantly in fear of being outlawed.

Let me say straight away that I am firmly in favour of pupils and teachers being exposed to a debate about 'profit' within the context of a capitalist or socialist society. The important change in perspective (say from Keith Joseph's) is due to the introduction of the word 'debate'. What is implied here is that the educator has the duty to introduce ideas, concepts and analyses in order to open up topics for debate and enable his or her pupil to achieve their own position, having made a thorough examination of the evidence. On most issues the teachers' own position will not be crucial but on some it would be so important that teacher and pupil find it difficult to work together. It follows that there should always be a right, firmly embedded in a well-understood charter of pupil rights, for a pupil to withdraw. (The teacher already has the power to exclude a pupil.) Clearly this would be seen as a device of the last resort. In most cases of radical conflict it should be possible, through openness and negotiation, to prevent withdrawal. Indeed, the process of working out how to cooperate in a learning process and bridge substantial differences in world view, would in itself be a valuable experience.

From this argument, it does not follow that the teacher should always be prepared to act as a neutral chairperson – as is prescribed by the 'humanities curriculum project'. Indeed, it would seem to me that this weakens teachers' pedagogic stance on two grounds.

1. It would not actually reflect the true position of the teacher (in most cases) and would, therefore, be seen either as a charade or a device.
2. It removes the possibility of the pupils to make judgements about the teacher, to point to inconsistencies and learn through their formal and informal experience of the person concerned.

In the end, the pupil can only be safeguarded by the principle of 'openness'. The teacher's view should be put forward, but in an open, challengeable way and should not be given more status than other views. If the pupil/parent finds that this is not the case they should be free to withdraw. On the other hand, if the pupil exhibits a view that the teacher (in the end) cannot accommodate, the pupil should be withdrawn.

I take this position for a number of reasons. The most important, however, is that I believe it is now crucial that education, in practice, extends its scope to include new areas of controversy and discord. Without this extension it will fail to engage the interests of young people and fail to inform them of the critically important issues which they will face in their lifetime.

The issue of 'bias', which faces any attempts at socialist education, can be further clarified by outlining the definition of socialism that I am using here. The definition of socialism and/or capitalism can be a long and complex business, but I will attempt to short-circuit this procedure without producing too much confusion and ambiguity.

Capitalism emerged in the 17th and 18th Centuries, firmly associated with individualism. Adam Smith (1890) was able to shape a theoretical justification of capitalism that has remained largely undisturbed to this day. According to Smith, capitalism developed, and capitalist economic organizations came into being, as individuals pursued profit maximization within the context of a free market. *The Wealth of the Nations* (1890) demonstrated that a nation where citizens were engaged in the pursuit of self-interest would be propelled forward much faster economically than other nations where traditional values or moral constraints prevented the pursuit of self-interest. This meant that the individual need not feel guilty about striving in his or her own interest. There was a social mechanism, 'the hidden hand', which ensured that the outcome was for the eventual benefit of all. The mechanism worked because the effect of economic growth, produced by profit maximization, would be far more beneficial to the poor of that country, than all the moral sentiment or traditional protection afforded them in less dynamic countries. It is clear that our present education system is largely shaped by this imperative – the emphasis on individual achievement, examinations and standards is clearly displayed.

Socialism, as a doctrine, emerged soon after capitalism. It is concerned centrally with equality and the collective or social interest, with replacing the free operation of the market with a more rational and planned set of goals. It is my view, that attempts at socialist development have failed, in most cases so far, to replace 'the market' with institutions and/or mechanisms that reflect the wishes of a progressively enlightened and discerning body of consumers.

On the other hand, capitalist systems of production have made extensive use of 'socialist' institutions to modify the differentiating effects of the 'free market' and the plague of social ills which accompany it. It follows that both socialists and the supporters of capitalism have an interest in developing dual strands within the present education system. The suppression of one strand, at the expense of the other, by pretending that 'education' is somehow value-free and divorced from the central issue of politics, is in fact, in our capitalist society, to indoctrinate education in a capitalist fashion. We have an indoctrinated education which is increasingly inadequate in the face of rapidly developing social, economic and ecological problems on a world scale.

The traditional argument for the replacement of capitalism by socialism, propounded by Marx but elaborated and adapted by socialists over the last 100 years, was based on the failure of capitalism to redistribute the fruits of the increasingly efficient technologically based industry, owned and controlled by capitalists. This, indeed, has remained an important problem, although it has shifted from being a problem largely associated with differentiation and stratification within a nation state, to differentiation and polarization between nation states. The progressive impoverishment of the Third World is now a major international problem which is incapable of solution within the mechanisms of the 'free market'. Less developed country (LDC) is a term which hides the fact that there will always be some countries excluded from the kind of development experienced by the Western capitalist countries. Some form of planned interference with the market, to move it in the direction of greater equality, and with the social or collective interest in mind, is inevitable if these problems are to be tackled. The question is, whether it will be an intelligent and effective set of initiatives based on a wide understanding of the problems, or a grudging, time saving, system-patching set of manoeuvres proposed by a small but dominant group within the Western democracies. The education system's response to these problems is, therefore, crucial.

The second major problem specifically related to modern capitalism, harnessed with modern technology, is paradoxically, technology's success. The massive power of our industrial culture means that we can ruthlessly exploit every natural environment, from the ice caps to the equator and from the ocean beds to outer space.

We have grown powerful with respect to nature and can destroy or decimate a major species or a major ecological zone almost without noticing it. The free play of individual self-interest is a poor basis from which to tackle these kinds of problems. It will always be in the individual's interest to exploit a diminishing natural resource – and this will continue – if others will not recognize the collective interest and need for rational planning. The mechanisms described by the phrases 'the tragedy of the commons' and the 'tyranny of small decisions' are well documented and clearly understood. This constitutes a second important reason why something like a 'socialist education' must start to make a major impression on our education system.

Where it has to Go Now
If We are Serious about Socialism

John Wright's recent article in the *New Statesman* (11.4.86) on 'Where it went wrong in the classroom' was a rare event in a socialist journal. It was a clear analysis of many of the problems associated with the 'progressive' education of the sixties and made a forward looking 'demand' that socialists begin to *think seriously* about education. This paper is an attempt to move the debate along and to involve others in thinking about a socialist education. I take seriously the argument that what must be addressed

> 'is the more fundamental task of defining a role which schools can play in the broader struggle to transform our society (and indeed the world) into something more humane, more equal.'

> (Wright, 1986)

For socialists, the possibility of progressively shaping the thoughts of future generations is of utmost importance. Yet, this aim is almost totally neglected. Except for the dedicated but isolated struggles of individual teachers in schools and other institutions there is almost no work being done on what might constitute a socialist education. The Labour Party's efforts in this direction are a disgrace. Apart from a few woolly ideas about more opportunity, more relevant skills and more comprehensiveness at various levels, there seems to be no more insight into a socialist curriculum or a socialist pedagogy than there was in 1945. In the absence of any convincing ideas from the left the centre stage of politics has been captured by the radical right. Not only have they succeeded in persuading the electorate that standards are the most important measure of our education system, but with the help of Jim Callaghan (1976) they have managed to slough off the responsibility for our industrial decline on to schools and universities. The multiple causes of our economic decline ranging from high interest rates, and the high value of the pound, to poor managerial skills and an alienated labour force, therefore, can be conveniently transformed into the failure of schools to produce students with high enough standards in the traditional skills of literacy and mathematics and more recently, with industrially relevant skills. The fact that such a wafer-thin argument could have carried the field speaks volumes for the quality of the opposition.

What is more amazing in the battle for education is that socialists find themselves defending totally inappropriate educational institutions; as though socialism had an umbilical connection with GCE 'O' levels, banded comprehensive schools and an outdated, traditional academic curriculum designed to encourage the promotion of an elite. The present school system discriminates against working class pupils, ethnic minority groups and female pupils. It fails to develop in children an understanding of the kinds of problems that they will need to confront in their lifetimes, either as individuals or collectively. In fact, many of the practices the education system encourages will lead them to undervalue their own abilities, neglect important skills and lead lives which are unnecessarily shortened and disfigured with ill-health. In short, far from encouraging creative energies, schools alienate many of their pupils and fail to educate.

It is because so many people realize that schools are failing them, that the Right has been able to attract such broad support for its critical stance on education. Right-wing arguments may be misleading and false, but they are the only critical assessment of education popularly available. It is, in an odd way, less insulting than the policies of the Labour left, which come across as saying that if you have more of this dreadful experience – expensive and alienating as it may be – things will get better.

It is important to notice that, while the analysis presented here directs attention to the inadequacies of the system, it does not 'blame the teachers'. My view is that teachers are the victims rather than the perpetrators of this misguided education. They feel as frustrated and embittered as their pupils and much of the determination and militancy that has flowed into their industrial action over the last two years stems from a deep discontent with the system in which they are entrapped. This is an important asset that the left could and should speedily harness. Teachers see themselves as sacrificial scapegoats, victims of the radical right's criticism of the system, which ends up by putting the blame firmly on the shoulders of inadequate teachers or of inadequate training for new teachers. In fact, despite the present industrial action concerning rights over wage negotiation and the former embargo on noncontractual activity, it is clear that large numbers of teachers would be willing to put large amounts of time and energy into enterprises and activities that would improve their schools and the education they offer. The findings of the Schools Council demonstrated, beyond any doubt, that what is usually missing in schools is the opportunity, the direction and necessary coordination of effort. The Council findings only scratch the surface of the energies entrapped and frittered away within schools. A socialist policy for education should aim to liberate these enormous

reserves of wasted energy and transform schools within a decade.
To do this it will need to

1. base its policy on a proper diagnosis of what is wrong with the
   present system;
2. point to obtainable goals and provide the resources to achieve
   them; and
3. establish the general principles of a socialist education within
   a broad, convincing, philosophical framework.

The first problem that must be clarified, therefore, is the
diagnosis of what is wrong with our schools and the education they
offer. Recent experiences of dissatisfaction and increasing
alienation within our schools have often been diagnosed in the
following ways: as resulting from falling rolls; diminishing
inadequate resources for schools and teacher remuneration;
diminished career prospects; and a sense of failure stemming from
increasing youth unemployment. These are important factors but
it is doubtful whether they represent the total answer.

Prior to its present-day contracted state, the education system
has been geared up to select and allocate each new generation
within a burgeoning economy. In the 30 years after World War
II the new expanding middle classes more than doubled. The
economy needed a supply of 'educated' recruits, who were suitable
for the expanding numbers and varieties of professional, technical
and managerial jobs. Schools, therefore, became the arena in
which the competition took place for the certificates that
guaranteed these new careers. They were distributed, however, on
the basis of a bogus meritocratic justice, shrouded in an ideology of
equality of opportunity. The competitive pressures within this
system have grown over the years and have absorbed more and
more of the energies of pupils, parents and teachers: for
examination pupils, about four years out of the six or seven years
of secondary schooling are now given almost entirely to
examination preparation. In practice, for most subjects, this
means the rote learning of overcrowded syllabi. For the children
who have 'lost out' in this competition, it means a devalued
education, drained of purpose and direction. This experience can
lead many in secondary education (40 per cent in ILEA) to regress
with respect to some of the basic accomplishments of the system –
literacy and numeracy. My own study of schools (Lacey, 1970) and
the work of many others (Hargreaves, 1967 and 1982; Woods,
1979; Ball, 1981) confirm the thesis that, an education system
based almost exclusively on individual competition leads to a

polarization among individuals making up the system and that a large number of pupils actually reject the values and skills the system seeks to teach. In addition, it is clear from the work of others (Goodson, 1983; Cooper, 1985; Young. 1971; Whitty, 1985) that in these circumstances the curriculum becomes increasingly rigid and overcrowded as examination pressures and preoccupation with success dominate the ideology of the school and also become a preoccupation of individual teachers looking to advance their 'careers'.

The research on which the above analysis is based, shows clearly that the education system had lost its way prior to the cuts and contraction of the mid-1970s. It had become, increasingly, a mechanism for social allocation in which the essentially critical and creative processes of education failed to develop. The crisis of the late seventies and early eighties has merely uncovered the lack of any development towards an adequate education. The extension of education through the Raising Of The School Leaving Age (ROSLA) and the increasing numbers staying on into the sixth form and further education can now be seen as a response to the competition for positions within the job market as 'qualification inflation' affected one educational certificate after another (Dawe, 1976). The achievement the Left made in expanding education can no longer be used in itself as an indicator of progress.

Conversations with pupils in our secondary schools can very rapidly reveal just how widespread the disillusionment and disenchantment has become. Even among the academic elite there are powerful mechanisms for distancing oneself from those few pupils identified as pro-school and enthusiastic. In one local comprehensive the current labels for this group among top band pupils include 'boffins', the 'the yahs' and 'creepy arse-licks'. The terms vividly demonstrate the phenomenon. The most striking feature about this rejection or distancing, however, is not its crudeness or militancy. It is often accompanied by an understanding and an awareness that brings into question the present status of pupils in schools, as illustrated by the following quotations:

'Many people around me genuinely feel qualifications will not bring better job prospects, whilst others use high unemployment as a scapegoat to justify laziness; either way, this pessimism of young people, which is part of the eighties, is working against the school.'

'Schools are microcosms of our society. Teachers are always looking for the lower class pupils to do wrong. They, when caught, are then punished accordingly.'

'If the aim of the education system is to ensure that a certain number of people pass certain exams every year, then yes, the education system is working. But exams are a continually declining currency. And we are losing a sense of moral and social values ... Terms such as "right" and "wrong" are now frowned upon. In fact, if we want the educational system to promote social reform it is not just important what is taught but how it is taught.'

'To call our system fair, equal and, to quote the Labour Party, "egalitarian", is a joke.'

'I attend a comprehensive school where financial restrictions are now starkly apparent ... Rarely now is a teacher replaced ... As a sixth former I now have to provide all paper, files and so on.'

These quotations are not from teachers or educationalists, they are from sixth formers who entered the *New Society* essay competition in 1984. They display the kinds of insight and understanding on which an education should build. The challenge for socialists is clear. It is to build an education which attracts support from teachers and parents because it engages their children and helps them confront the growing array of problems that face them and their generation. The new education must provide a series of creative opportunities for pupils to identify problems, acquire the skills and information necessary to attempt a solution and the freedom and space to bring their intelligence to bear on those problems.,

The next stage is to establish a set of achievable policy goals which will establish the structural conditions for a socialist education. The analysis outlined above already suggests one necessary condition for success. This is that *it will be necessary to limit and fence-off the central competitive, examination-centred process that currently afflicts education*. This could be done in a number of ways ranging from abolition of the '16+', suggested by David Hargreaves (1982), to the more modest proposal of limiting the number of '16+' examinations it is possible to take and also limiting the amount of time that any school can legally spend on them within the curriculum.

Any reform of this kind would have immediate repercussions on higher education and recruitment to jobs. It would almost certainly fail to establish the conditions necessary for 'education' to proceed after school, without corresponding reforms affecting job opportunities – through job sharing and job creation – and the expansion and reform of higher and further education. A socialist education policy, therefore, must be coordinated with a series of reforms involving the examination system, job opportunities, further education and new kinds of work (for example, in cooperatives, or in social and community work).

The problem of creating fertile external conditions for a democratic socialist education is one thing. The effort involved in building the positive, in living and developing experience within institutions presently so remote from democratic socialism, is quite another matter. First and foremost, there is a need to create more open, egalitarian and democratic structures within schools. These reforms are needed both within the staff-room and in teacher/pupil relations. At present, five levels of scale post and additional layers within the teaching 'hierarchy', produce a rigidity and lack of democracy that is difficult to reconcile with a learning institution: proposed changes to the system will do little to alter this. The structure is reminiscent of the army. The responsibility of young people for their own learning must be recognized centrally and in law, and should not be placed in authoritarian pupil/school councils (where they exist). Pupils need a structure or framework within which they make important decisions about *their* curriculum and within which the school can be expected to respond helpfully and learn by responding.

Once the problems of achieving a democratic structure and new goals within schools have been solved; the next problem concerns resources. The question of resources must take the needs of the learning process as its top priority. This does not mean that teachers' salaries or the effects of educational expenditure on the economy should be neglected, but that resources for teacher study leave and time for project development should amount to a sizeable part of the budget of every school. Any system that does not plough back at least 10 per cent of its energies (money and time) for renewal is asking for decline and breakdown in the long run.

The final, and in many ways central, questions to be debated relate to pedagogy and curriculum content. These are also the most neglected and avoided issues. The Left has been neutralized by fear of being accused of indoctrination or of being blamed for the politicizing of education. This has thus allowed the right to launch an onslaught on peace studies, health education and anything else that deviates from their educational ideology and their view of the needs of industry. In so doing, the right has politicized education and there can be no return to the 'innocence' of the past. There are powerful arguments that socialists can muster concerning the 'right to know' in a world society that is now tottering on the edge of so many man-made disasters. The 'new' generations must be equipped with knowledge of the dangers that will face them. Quite apart from the practical issue of seeking solutions, there is the moral question of the right to participate in decisions that in many spheres have become life threatening. The issues I have in mind extend from ecological problems, on the scale of the destruction of the Amazon jungle with its likely concomitants of climatic change and desertification, to the issue of worldwide economic polarization where, on the one hand one nation with 7 per cent of the world's population absorbs 35 per cent of the world's resources, while the least developed countries have an average annual income of about $150 per head (Brandt Report, 1980). They also include issues like the 'arms race', nuclear power energy generation, space exploration and the effects of fast-food and food additives on the teenage diet. The job of a socialist education in these areas is to inform young people of the problems and issues and encourage them to develop the skills and knowledge they need to make their own judgements about the future – hardly a blue-print for indoctrination.

The systematic study of important issues, using the strengths of established disciplines, should become the core of a socialist education. The two phases of this education, 'critical education' and 'constructive education' provide a framework in which questions can be explored and possible solutions examined in ways that relate to the real world and to the concerns of young people.

Therefore, our new education system would resemble twin tracks of equal importance. One track would be similar to our present system of discipline-centred education, where individuals would obtain a grounding in a wide range of disciplines, but would then specialize in a few. The second track (the core), would be a problem-centred curriculum in which individuals collaborated in the analysis of problems and in constructing solutions to them. Some of the problems would be of a theoretical nature; others of a practical or technical nature; some would involve skills of organization and person-centred skills while others would call upon an artistic and creative imagination. The groups (and individuals) tackling these problems would share their thoughts and achievements with others via workshops and conferences. The concepts of critical and constructive education, therefore, are central to the idea of a socialist education and deserve to be examined further.

Postscript: Critical and Constructive Education Examined

The argument for a socialist education rests on two arguments about relevance. The first proposes a form of education that is non-doctrinaire and relevant to our current 'mixed' economy. The second proposes a form of education that is relevant to the future and capable of research and redirection as the problems facing our society change and become more acute. Despite the potency of these arguments, the real test for any proposal concerning education is whether it can be developed in a form that is capable of being deployed within the school and the classroom. The political battle over limiting the time and scope for traditional examinations can only begin if teachers, parents and pupils are convinced that they possess an alternative curriculum and pedagogy that will work. They need to feel sure that it is a practical proposition which teachers can operate without an impossible outlay of energy or an unrealistically high level of talent.

The proposal I make for critical and constructive education is based on my experience of teaching which ranges from MA work accomplished by teachers at university level, to teaching in secondary modern and comprehensive schools and also includes my study of my own children's education and the monitoring of teaching carried out by PGCE (Post Graduate Certificate of Education) students in training. It is essentially a set of proposals gleaned from a life-time involvement with teaching and based on my experience of the practical, day-to-day world. Critical and constructive education involves a set of teaching strategies that I have developed in a partial and patch-work way within my own career, and more importantly, that I have seen begin to emerge within the work of many others: whether they be newly-qualified teachers, teachers working within curriculum development projects (see Huckle and Whitty, Chapters 2.3 and 2.4, within this book), teachers working in school based projects or individual teachers experimenting within their own classrooms. In other words, this set of proposals is based on a broad strand of endeavour that is already occurring. It needs to be recognized and adopted into a culture of teaching and interest groups concerned with issues relating to development, the environment and other strategic issues. Only if these developments take place and these connections are made will education be able to drag itself free from its impediments and constraints and contribute to the problem of social and ecological renewal.

Critical education

The purpose behind critical education is not destructive. It is not an excuse to vent one's spleen or engage in self-glorification at the expense of others who are being criticized. The intention is exactly the opposite. Critical education should lead to deeper understanding and the possibility of constructive action and development. If it is not encountered with this purpose in mind it can give rise to unnecessary conflict and wasted energy. The essential skill within the discipline of critical education is to establish which elements from the previous educational construction are sound and also relevant to the purpose in hand. In this way, a necessary base can be built and the preliminary elements of a methodology established, which will point the way towards a means of obtaining the new goal.

Stated in this way critical education would seem to be an extension of common sense. Who would embark on any undertaking, large or small, safe or perilous, without undertaking this preliminary critical appraisal? Why should an education system give such emphasis to something that anyone in their right mind would undertake as a matter of course? The answer to these questions establishes the importance of critical education. The sad fact is that all kinds of self-interested considerations social constraints and personal limitations come between the ideal of critical appraisal and the practice of construction.

One interesting example of a critical education exercise was recently completed by a group of MA students at Sussex University. Their task was to explore critically the cultural hero Captain Falcon Scott using two main sources; The Ladybird book on *Captain Scott* written by L. du Garde Peach, (OBE, MA, PhD Litt) and a book written by Roland Huntford, *The Last Place on Earth*.

Peach's book was specifically written for children of junior school age and has had a very wide circulation. We find that Scott's expedition is described as:

'One of the most gallant ventures in the history of our race. Courage, determination, the highest sense of duty were defeated by the worst weather of the most savage climate of the world.'

The story is simply told with the occasional purple paragraph and the very occasional mention of Amundsen:

'The Norwegian, Amundsen, was well on his way to the Pole by an easier route.'

It is a modern version of Scott's 'adventure'.

Using Roland Huntford's text as a basis for comparison it was possible for the students to find 22 half-truths or complete untruths and a large number of important omissions. For example, Scott:

1. *Failed* to realize that eating fresh meat was the only easy way of preventing scurvy (this was the reason that Amundsen's party ate their dogs). Scott probably died of scurvy.

2. *Failed* to understand and make proper use of dogs and skis. Instead he punished himself and his men by overwork with inadequate rations.
3. *Failed* to plan adequately the logistic supply and packaging of food and fuel. As a result they lost paraffin through fuel creep and ran out of their supply of food.
4. *Wasted* time through poor navigation and poor marking of food and fuel bases.
5. *Failed* to take adequate clothing and tents (the tents had no sewn-in ground sheet).

This list contains less than one quarter of the major shortcomings of the Scott expedition. It reveals that Scott did not undertake the 'critical exercise' outlined above and, as a result, failed to learn from the recorded experience lodged in a library close to his London office. In addition, he set up an authoritarian, hierarchical organization that prevented an upward flow of information from men who knew the answers to many of the incredible mistakes he made. He set up an organization which imprisoned its members, and by not drawing on their skills and knowledge it rendered them less intelligent in the face of the problems they encountered. It caused four of them to die. A book which fails to draw these lessons from the expedition, renders its readers less intelligent. It bolsters prejudice, misinforms and spreads the kind of self-righteous complacency for which the English are famous.

The exercise also drew on information from Amundsen's expedition. The contrast was extreme. Amundsen led an expedition which was run as a 'little republic'. He invited open discussion, accepted advice from 'expert' colleagues and gave them room to develop and apply their skills. They:

1. Lightened the best sledges by 50lbs.
2. Used eskimo clothing.
3. Learned eskimo methods for driving dogs.
4. Learned eskimo methods for building igloos.

Amundsen had lived with a family of eskimos in order to learn these things. They also:

5. Designed wind proof tents with sewn-in ground sheets.
6. Developed snow tunnelling for their stores at base camp.
7. Ate dog meat to prevent scurvy.
8. Packed their stores in such a way that the sledges could remain packed while overnight rations were removed.

9. Took decisions democratically (they voted on whether to go to the South Pole).

They used a comradely, purposeful (happy) organization which was designed for learning and for sharing experience. They only needed to travel between 9.00 am and 1.00 pm, but they still beat Scott's far larger, more expensive 'circus' by several weeks.

The student group then went on to discuss whether schools resembled Scott's expedition or Amundsen's. To their surprise (and horror) they came to the conclusion that they were generally closer to Scott's undemocratic, hierarchical model, which rendered participants less intelligent. The account of this exercise led almost inevitably to proposals for exercises in constructive education.

Constructive education

Critical education can develop the facility for forming frameworks of understanding or systematic understanding. It is, however, limited to this function. On its own it cannot yield the fruits of experience and it cannot deliver the results of experimentation. This element of praxis, of direct personal involvement with problems, can be provided by constructive education. This form of education is not to be confused with practical education – education which takes place in a workshop or laboratory (although workshops and laboratories can provide excellent opportunities for constructive education and modern approaches to CDT (craft, design and technology) come very close to it). In practical lessons, in most of our schools, the essential elements of construction have been removed. Nearly all the decisions about what is to be done and how it is to be organized have been taken in advance by the teacher, so that little remains for the pupil beyond following the cook-book instructions and making sure he or she gets the 'right' answer. The whole process has usually been streamlined to speed the process of learning (of facts) so that very little construction remains. So much time is presently spent in cramming pre-ordained facts into pupils' heads that little is learned about the process of constructing a solution to a problem.

The contrast provided by the Scott and Amundsen expeditions is most marked on this issue. Scott's organization and procedure was imported wholesale from the British Navy – the hierarchy, the separation of status, the downward flow of instructions coupled with an intolerance of the upward flow of criticism and counter suggestions – all were characteristics developed in a situation where predictability, certainty and control were expected to be at a premium. It was assumed that the greatest knowledge and ability resided at the top of the hierarchical structure (Burns and Stalker, 1961). In the uncertain circumstances of polar travel a great deal had to be learned. The kind of organization required for this task was almost the opposite of that used by Scott. It needed to be open to relevant experience and expertise. It has been shown that to achieve this openness it was necessary to reduce hierarchical and status difference. People must be approached on the basis of their skill, or their contribution to the problem in hand, not according to some predetermined differentiation based on other factors. In addition people who are consulted need to feel:

1. Confident that their voice will be heard and that it is, therefore, worthwhile concerning themselves with problems outside a narrow definition of their role. That is, they need to develop a concern for the whole and they will only do this if they see a possibility of making use of the knowledge acquired in their own specialist role.
2. That it is right or legitimate that they should be consulted. Individuals should not feel that others, because they have more status or more reward, should be solely responsible for solving problems.

Constructive education should allow pupils to explore solutions to these kinds of problem and to become familiar with the strengths and weaknesses of many kinds of organization. The scope of constructive education should extend into any problem area that pupils and teachers wish to confront. Some of these problems will have technological solutions, others resource solutions, but increasingly pupils will come to see that a large number of problems are open to solution through the organization of already existing social resources (whether these be expensively maintained butter-mountains or under-utilized resources in schools).

Clearly, issues relating to development and ecology are central to the task of building a relevant content for both critical and constructive education. The modern world poses problems for young people and future generations that were unknown and unanticipated in earlier generations. These young people will require an awareness and skill in educating themselves to confront these problems, that can only be described as a new kind of intelligence. They will need to be in control of their own life-styles and capable of rapid responsive collective action to problems that emerge with frightening rapidity. It is only necessary to consider the diagnosis and spread of 'AIDS' to illustrate the kind of problem that 'our' generation will bequeath to 'their' generation. If we add to this picture, the issues raised in this book relating to 'inner' and 'outer' ecology, then the range of problems appears as an almost frightening vista. Coupled with the problems of the relationship between the first, second and third worlds and the destructive elements in those relationships that the developed countries seem to foster in order to maintain their advantage, the scope for effective action would seem to be limited. Despite the immensity of the task I still remain optimistic about *homo sapiens'* ability to respond. There are still large reservoirs of imagination and creative energy to be tapped. The key to these energies lies within the new intelligence described above and much now depends on our ability to organize our education system so that it engages with the 'real' problems and releases new critical and constructive energies to combat them.

References

Ball, S. (1981) *Beachside Comprehensive*. Cambridge University Press.

Brandt Report (1980) *North–South: A Programme for Survival*. Pan Books.

Burns, T. and Stalker, G. (1961) *The Management of Innovation*. Tavistock Press, London.

Callaghan, J. (1976) Ruskin College Speech. *Times Educational Supplement*, October.

Cooper, B. (1985) *Renegotiating Secondary School Mathematics*. Falmer Press.

Danse, R. (1976) *The Diploma Disease*. George Allen and Unwin, London.

du Garde Peach, L. (1963) *Captain Scott*. Ladybird books.

Goodson, I. (1983) *School Subjects and Curriculum Change*. Croom Helm.

Hargreaves, D. (1967) *Social Relations in a Secondary School*, (1982) *The Challenge for the Comprehensive School*. Routledge and Kegan Paul, London.

Huntford, R. (1979) *The Last Place on Earth*. Hodder and Stoughton.

Lacey, C. (1970) *Hightown Grammar*. Manchester University Press.

Smith, A. (1890) *The Wealth of Nations*. George Allen and Unwin, London.

Woods, P. (1979) *The Divided School*. Routledge and Kegan Paul, London.

Whitty, G. (1985) *Sociology and School Knowledge*. Methuen.

Wright, J. (1986) 'Where it went wrong in the classroom'. In *New Statesman*, 11 April.

Young, M. (ed.) *Knowledge and Control*. Collins Macmillan, London.

Chapter 2.2

EDUCATIONAL ASSESSMENT – A TEST FOR SOCIALISM

Andrew Hargreaves,
Department of Education,
University of Warwick

In British secondary schools, few matters concern and preoccupy those who teach and those who are taught more than educational assessment – especially in the form of public examinations. Pupils work hard to pass them. Teachers measure their own and their colleagues' competence by them. Much of the curriculum is geared towards them, and parents and politicians judge the performance of schools in terms of them. As Patricia Broadfoot (1979, 1984) puts it, examinations therefore attest to *competence*; they organize curriculum *content*; they stimulate and regulate *competition*, and they maintain overall *control* over educational development and change (or its absence). Clearly, secondary school examinations have a powerful and wide-ranging set of functions and effects within the modern educational system.

Why is it, then, that the Labour movement, and the Left more generally, have apparently taken such little interest in public examinations, or indeed, in assessment as a whole? Why has assessment been largely absent from the Left's policy agenda on education? Further, what might the consequences of such continuing neglect be for educational development under socialist or social-democratic leadership? And what positive steps towards bringing about change in educational assessment might usefully be adopted in the future that would be consistent with socialist policy and practice? This chapter raises issues that might stimulate discussion about these questions.

The Neglect of Assessment

The Left and the Labour Party in particular never really seems to have grasped the nettle of examination or assessment reform. Proposals for reform did feature in the Great Debate in the mid-1970s, but quickly subsided. Discussions about common examining at 16+ also took place under Shirley Williams' ministership but these were drawn out and indecisive – diverted first to the Waddell committee which reported in 1978, then overtaken by a General Election. In part, this indecision was almost certainly due to delaying tactics by the Department of Education and Science (DES); to its attempts to defer decisions about this vital and influential area of educational policy until it (rather than the teacher-dominated Schools Council) could establish a firmer grip on the policy-making process (Salter and Tapper, 1987). But in some measure, the indecision was also due to Labour's lack of conviction about, and commitment to, examination reform of a radical nature (Whitty, 1985).

By contrast, Conservatives have accorded central importance to assessment in their policy agenda. The introduction of the new General Certificate of Secondary Education (GCSE) at almost breakneck speed; the inauguration of the Certificate of Pre-Vocational Education (CPVE) as a way of linking credentials to the burgeoning curriculum developments in vocational education; the growth of graded tests and assessments in particular subject areas; the institution of 'Records of Achievement' for all at 16 by the end of the 1980s; the requirement that schools publish their examination results, ostensibly to assist parents in choosing schools for their children. These are some of the most significant educational reforms that have been introduced over the recent years. They are reforms which, in their scope and in their speed of implementation, signal the Conservative Government's keen awareness of assessment as a dominant influence upon the curriculum, and as something over which central government is able to exert relatively direct control in the furtherance of its own educational and political ambitions.

The response of the Left, and the Labour movement generally, has been disappointing. They have, of course, complained about the under-resourcing and over-hasty implementation of the GCSE. Less strongly, they have also expressed reservations about the maintenance of differentiated levels of entry within the new examination. And, especially within the teacher unions, they have voiced anxieties about the financing and staffing of new assessment developments overall (Roy, 1987). Such are the worries that underpin the most common objection to assessment reform – 'Where is all the time going to come from?' Aside from complaints about general levels of staffing and resourcing, though, the Left has had very little to say about the educational or social desirability of the newly emerging patterns of assessment – about profiles, graded assessments, the national criteria for GCSE etc. Nor has it outlined, in any detail, what patterns of assessment would be compatible with a specifically socialist approach to education. On these matters concerning the general purpose and character of educational assessment, the Left's voice has been disappointingly mute.

In a Fabian pamphlet outlining Labour education policy for the next election and in a key speech, by Labour's shadow Education Minister, Giles Radice (1986); the Party has committed itself to an ambitious programme of reform and expansion. Expansion of access to further and higher education, better remuneration for teachers, more resources for books and buildings, redirection of state resources and support from the private to the state sector, and so forth. All this is couched in an urgent but optimistic language of expansion, opportunity and investment in human potential.

After a long period of serious retrenchment in educational expenditure, it is likely that the restoration of firm commitments to improve access, expansion and opportunity will be a popular move. At the same time, one cannot help feeling that socialist thinking should really be moving further than this – into the no-longer 'secret garden' of the curriculum which the Conservatives have increasingly made their own and landscaped to their own taste and design; and into the related areas of educational assessment too. In many respects, it was the failure of Labour (and the Left more generally) to develop a broad, popular and distinctively socialist set of policies on curriculum and assessment that helped remove the party from government. Its policies of access and expansion were no longer tenable in the midst of the 1970s recession (Hargreaves, 1986a). Furthermore, the preference for reform by administrative means seemed less and less relevant as the bulk of comprehensive reorganization was completed (Simon, 1985).

The Conservatives had already seized the initiative on the issues of standards, quality and the curriculum. When Labour *did* reluctantly enter the debate about the content and process of education, most notably through James Callaghan's Ruskin College speech and the Great Debate that followed it, for want of a clearly thought through and broadly agreed socialist view of the *process* of education, all that could be offered was a pale replica of Conservative thinking – the need to tighten up the relationship between school and working life, to give more attention to basic skills, and so forth.

Are we, I wonder, in danger of repeating this error, of meeting the educational challenges of the eighties with the solutions of the sixties? Of course, the case for expanded resourcing and equalizing of opportunities in education is strong now, and whatever policies are ultimately adopted relating to the content and process of education, they will require an adequate infrastructure of human and material resources if they are to be carried out effectively. But what will happen when the brief expansionist honeymoon is over? What policies will the Left then have to offer on education?

So far, the extent of Labour's commitments in the area of assessment policy appears to be a twin pledge, to remove the differentiated levels of entry in the GCSE and, to couple this academic qualification with more vocationally orientated ones like the CPVE into a unified examination system. The Socialist Education Association (1986) wishes to encourage more emphasis on course work assessment and profile reporting, but these ideas are not really elaborated upon. Similarly, Giles Radice's Fabian Pamphlet contains only one paragraph on educational assessment up to 16. It argues:

> 'Existing public examinations, even the new GCSE exam, assess only some of the skills which pupils need to develop. They also place too little emphasis on continuous assessment and project work. The pursuit of higher standards will require more broadly based assessment systems, including pupil profiles and records of achievement.'

(Radice, 1986:12)

The pamphlet then goes on to advocate modular approaches to study with pupils being assessed at the end of each six-to-eight week module so that they would 'have something to show for their efforts'. None of this, it should be said, is recognizably different from approaches to educational assessment that have been developed under, and with the support of, the Conservative Government. Many of the Conservatives' new assessment initiatives, therefore, have been tacitly endorsed by Labour. Beyond all this, it is simply suggested that assessment policy (and now a national curriculum too) be left to be developed by a broadly constituted Education Council and a newly defined inspectorate. Indeed, Giles Radice has even said that the existing GCSE might provide a useful basis for further developments of this kind. On the one hand, this deferral and delegation of important educational policy decisions might be interpreted as a reinvestment of political faith in and respect for the professional judgement of teachers and others closely involved in education. It might, however, equally be interpreted as setting aside political judgement and guidance on the content and process of education in a socialist society, or as a concern to avoid arousing hostility among sensitive parts of the electorate. Which of these is the case? This in turn raises the more general question – why neglect assessment?

Why neglect assessment?

There are, it seems to me, at least three possible reasons why assessment is currently downgraded as a feature of socialist education policy. First, assessment, at least in the shape of public examinations, has commonly been associated among wide sections of the public with standards, fairness and opportunity (Gray *et al* 1983). Radical policies of examination reform put these notions and political support for them at risk. Such policies can either threaten to downgrade allegedly rigorous forms of assessment with 'CSE-type' modes of examining, or if they involve abolition, they can threaten to replace public, objective and fair forms of selection with processes of selection that are private, subjective and unfair.

Secondly, clear government guidelines, or even starting points for discussion on assessment and indeed on curriculum, smack of centralism and of those bureaucratic intrusions upon teacher professionalism and individual judgement which have occasioned such strong resentment among teachers and LEAs under the present Government (Ranson and Tomlinson, 1986). The presentation of new policy guidelines on assessment, therefore, risks alienating not only parents with their concerns for standards and fairness, but the teacher unions too, concerned as they are to restore some dignity and public influence to the judgements and wishes of their profession.

Thirdly, in modern societies which continue to be characterized in some measure by economic and social inequalities, examinations and assessment in general are closely intertwined with the business of educational and social selection. This places socialist educational reformers in a number of apparently awkward dilemmas. If they present proposals for abolition of examinations at 16+, say, not only is this likely to arouse hostility among ambitious parents keen to retain a public and fair contest in which their children can compete; but it also begs the important question of what forms of assessment might be developed instead. This is perhaps why even some of the most ardent Left abolitionists (for example, Whitty, 1985) as yet appear to have no clear policy proposals concerning alternatives to examinations. On the other hand, if socialists propose more minor adjustments to, or reforms in the assessment system, they can then be accused of merely tinkering with, adjusting, perhaps even making more efficient, the existing process of educational selection – a task and set of purposes that is very much out of tune with the Left's equality ethic. Pupil profiles and records of achievement have been particularly open to these sorts of charges (Simon, 1985; Hargreaves, 1986b; Hargreaves *et al*, 1987, Broadfoot, 1986).

It may be, then, that the Left's and especially Labour's caution about setting out proposals for new patterns of educational assessment is as much to do with maintaining confidence among standards-conscious parents, respecting the professional sensitivities of the LEAs and the teacher unions, and reassuring its own supporters about its commitments to equality, as it is to do with any confidence in the future professional deliberations of the proposed Education Council. But are such cautions entirely necessary?

It is vital that the Left has a detailed policy on educational assessment for several reasons. First, parents' cause for concern that educational selection at 16 remains open, objective and fair in the form of public examinations, only retains its credibility if many young people directly enter paid employment at 16. Once direct entry to employment is deferred beyond 16, as the case is in many Western European countries, the acute need for an objective and rapidly processable sorting device is removed. In actual fact, in Britain we are currently experiencing a situation where less and less young people move directly into work at 16, but continue with some kind of further education or training instead. Perhaps we might now usefully consider making this situation, which is increasingly a matter of fact, into a situation of legal statute. Perhaps we should extend the period of education and training up to 17 for all in the first instance, and bring it within a common framework where opportunities for course access and for movement between courses and programmes are maximized to the fullest possible extent.

One way that progress through this system might be managed, is by a process of continuous course review, where continuous records and statements of achievement and course completion are passed through different parts of the system. No doubt, for some years there will still be a need for public certificates at 17 or beyond, but by deferring selection beyond 16, useful space will be afforded for curriculum change and the development of alternative forms of assessment before that point. This would give the secondary curriculum and the processes of teaching and learning that go on within it, the kind of breathing space necessary for development and innovation, which the primary schools enjoyed when the 11+ was abolished.

A second reason is that sensitivity about heavy-handed intrusion upon teachers' professional judgement and autonomy might, and perhaps should, deter educational policy makers from imposing new assessment policies by legal dictate, without the benefits of broad consultation with those who share in the educational partnership. However, in its reluctance to pre-empt professional dialogue, there is no reason why the Labour Party and the Labour movement should deliberately hide its political light under a consultative bushel. The political movement of socialism forms an important part of the educational partnership and it is proper that however open to modification and amendment its views on assessment might be later on, those views should be declared at the outset – in a discussion document perhaps – as part of a process of open, rigorous and vigorous debate. This means, of course, that the Left will need to think through its own views on assessment long before any new Education Council sets about its work.

Third, while assessment is often turned to the purpose of educational selection, it must be recognized that it also serves other valuable, indeed indispensable educational purposes. At its best, assessment can aid diagnosis of learning difficulties, enable teachers to identify strengths and weaknesses in their own teaching; give pupils feedback on their own learning and help them improve it; and (in the form of self-assessment) help pupils become more aware of and responsible for their own learning – discussing and negotiating it with their teachers where appropriate. In these senses, assessment is not just a way of ranking and rating the products of learning, but is an integral part of the learning process itself. Even the most ardent abolitionists, keen to eradicate all traces of selection from the educational system, must come to terms with these other purposes of assessment and consider their educational and social value.

A socialist assessment policy, then, does not end with the abolition of public examinations. Nor should a policy on assessment reform be overlooked if the abolitionist anti-selective goal turns out to be not immediately feasible. Assessment serves many other important social and educational purposes as well as selective ones, and the Left needs to think through its position in relation to them.

These, then, are the reasons why it is defensible, indeed vital for the Left to have a detailed and carefully worked out policy on educational assessment. I would now like to outline some issues that might merit consideration as part of such a policy within three broad assessment areas: public examinations, graded tests and assessments, and pupil profiles and records of achievement.

Public Examinations

One issue concerning a widely held claim about examinations, is that they are held to be responsible for a number of common ills in the teaching and learning process. It is said that they lead to didactic teaching, cramming, over-emphasis on dictation and written work and to a lack of group work and opportunities for the exercise of individual initiative (Her Majesty's Inspectorate, 1979; D. Hargreaves, 1982; Hitchcock, 1986). Interestingly, though, while the claim is a common one and has virtually reached the status of becoming accepted 'fact', supportive evidence in educational research findings is not strong. In explaining their preference for didactic methods, there is limited evidence that teachers *do* sometimes invoke examinations as a constraint or an excuse (Sikes, Measor and Woods, 1985), though for many teachers, exams are neither a welcome incentive nor an oppressive constraint, but simply part of the assumed background or 'facts of life' teaching (Scarth, 1983). Observational evidence in research carried out at the Open University, however, indicates that the proportions of time allocated to open and closed questions do not appear to be associated with whether the courses are examined, not-examined or examined by different modes (Hammersley and Scarth, 1986; Scarth and Hammersley, 1986). These findings may not, however, reflect differences that are important to teachers. To teachers, it may be no surprise at all that public classroom talk does not differ greatly between examination and non-examination classes. Indeed, such talk may be highly closed and teacher-dominated in classes using a lot of group work, since the purpose of that talk is to deliver instructions and report back on more open-ended tasks set on a small group basis. It could be, then, that Hammersley and Scarth have chosen to measure differences that are of little consequence for the examination debate (Woods, forthcoming). Even if it *could* be shown that differences between individual teachers were not great, this would still not demonstrate that examinations had no effect on teaching. What comparisons between teachers cannot really show is the extent to which the culture of examinations and examining exerts an influence upon the secondary school system as a whole, the breadth of the examination based curriculum and its dominant styles of teaching (D. Hargreaves, 1982).

The force of the influence exerted by examinations can be overstated though. Observational work on teaching styles in the United States of America – a nation with a very different pattern of assessment than Britain – reveals strikingly similar preferences for didactic, teacher-centred or 'frontal' patterns of teaching (Tye, 1985). This suggests that many other factors are responsible for didactic teaching as well as the constraints of public examinations (A. Hargreaves, forthcoming). Factors such as a preoccupation with the necessities of classroom control (Denscombe, 1985); a tendency for teachers to favour whole class teaching within particular subjects such as modern languages (Evans, 1985; Ball, 1981); the rooting of teachers by biographical habit to styles and patterns they have developed earlier in their careers, in grammar schools or tough secondary moderns, perhaps (Hargreaves, 1986a); or the way in which poor career prospects or opportunities 'spoilt' by reorganization or amalgamation can lead teachers to lower the effort and commitment they give to producing classroom excellence (Riseborough, 1981). It should not be assumed, therefore (as the promoters of the GCSE have done), that examination reform or abolition will automatically reduce the amount of influence of didactic teaching within the secondary school system. It will simply offer some opportunity for further reform initiatives to be developed with some hope of success. That is all.

Indeed, reforming the style of examination may influence teaching styles very little if the institution of public examinations persists as such, whatever their form. Particularly relevant here are the findings of some research into the effects of examination reform on teaching and learning processes in the classroom, long before the advent of GCSE. Research on integrated science, for instance, indicated that while the new curriculum and examination structure for this initiative officially discouraged formal revision and teaching 'from the front', nevertheless, that is precisely what teachers usually did in order, as they saw it, to maximize their classes' chances of success (Olson, 1983; Weston, 1979). Similarly, research on 'Schools Council History', a project whose criteria and patterns of assessment are fairly close to those which have been embodied in the new GCSE, has suggested that teachers respond to the criteria very differently depending on how they themselves perceive the nature of teaching history, the patterns of teaching to which they have become accustomed through previous experience, the way in which they get pupils through large quantities of material in the short time available, etc (Scarth, 1987). As the research shows, this can lead to wide variations in teaching new curricula and managing new patterns of assessment even in the same school.

One should not assume, therefore, that even when new, more pupil-centred learning criteria are built into a reshaped examination structure such as the GCSE that this will automatically produce the expected shifts in pattern of teaching and learning at classroom level. The continuing presence of public examinations, as such, whatever their form, and the persistence of all the other factors which encourage didactic teaching may together conspire to inhibit the widespread development of those new teaching styles which the GCSE is seeking to encourage. The hopes and the fears of those who have viewed GCSE as a way of manipulating teachers to adopt new styles of approach (eg Nuttall, 1984) therefore, may be exaggerated. Teachers are not manipulated that easily. Their isolation in the classroom still offers them considerable protection.

The second major issue concerns the restrictive effects of examinations on the curriculum. For socialist education policy, an important criticism is that public examinations lead to an over-emphasis on intellectual-cognitive skills to the detriment of practical, social and personal ones; to the dominance of mainstream traditional subjects where written work predominates and knowledge can easily be regurgitated (D. Hargreaves, 1982; ILEA, 1984). The emphases that public examinations give to and reinforce in the secondary curriculum make it difficult for new subjects like environmental education to establish themselves without becoming examined (Goodson, 1983). They make it difficult for marginal subjects like personal and social education to gain a status and recognition among teachers and pupils, equivalent to that of other secondary school subjects (Baglin, 1984; Burgess, 1984). They also make it difficult for marginalized areas of the curriculum like development education and political education to retain their relevance and social importance, their emphases on discussion and decision-making, without being converted into just another area of academic study with written work and an examination needed at the end in order to enhance their reputation and status. In this respect, it is significant that within the context of the present public examination system, even the relatively radical ILEA Report *Improving Secondary Schools* (1984) advises that the subject, personal and social education, be formally examined so as to increase its credibility. More important than the influence examinations have on teaching styles, then, is the restrictive effect they exert upon the school curriculum. They inhibit breadth or range of educational study. Such breadth, acquaintance with a wide range of subjects and experience of different kinds of educational achievement, operates in the interest of socialism; as right wing advocates of the removal of peace education, world studies, political education and the like from the curriculum, fully recognize (e.g. Scruton *et al*, 1985; Cox and Scruton, 1984). A narrow and conventional subject based curriculum with little relevance to issues of contemporary human importance where critical judgement and social awareness might otherwise be developed, serves conservative interests. In this sense, the appropriate response to a partisan, restricted, traditional, subject-based curriculum, is not an alternative, equally partisan one organized around specifically working-class interests (CCCS, 1981). Rather the response should be a broad curriculum – one which widens the scope of social and environmental awareness, arouses emotions of human concern and deepens the powers of critical judgement. Anything which restricts genuine curricular breadth and balance is, in this sense, a threat to the development and realization of socialist education policy. It is for this reason that reduction of the impact and influence of public examinations on the curriculum ought perhaps to be a key feature of Left policy on education.

The proposed introduction of national blanket testing of performance, in a range of what have been termed 'basic subjects', at ages 7, 11 and 14 presents particularly strong threats to the kind of curricular breadth and balance that is compatible with socialist and democratic interests. The restriction of the definition 'basic' to the conventional academic subjects of the grammar school curriculum such as English, mathematics and science ensures that because these things will be tested, and schools and teachers likely be held accountable by the results, this is where schools and teachers will commit most of their time and energy. Little time and opportunity will be left for the study of environmental education, political education and the like. And where coverage is given to such areas, they will be, as untested and therefore 'non-basic' parts of the curriculum, accorded less status and priority among teachers, pupils and parents too. Their marginalization will be accelerated still further. It is quite possible of course, that such marginalization might well be part of the political intention underlying this assessment initiative. Is it not far better to have teachers and schools themselves squeeze socially threatening elements off the curriculum as a result of more general government reforms in assessment, than risk ideological con-troversy and accusations of bias and partisanship, by making these parts of the curriculum an overt and open subject for political argument and confrontation?

At the time of writing, the Left, and the National Union of Teachers in particular, is resisting the proposal for periodic national testing. What it is not contesting, though, is the equally important issue of what subjects might legitimately be regarded as 'basic' in the first place. Is not political education 'basic' within a democratic society, for instance? What is basic and what is marginal – socialists and other democrats should not collude in perpetuating existing conventional understandings of these categories, but should make them the subject of active contestation in their educational policy agenda.

The GCSE also has special importance here. By the setting of national criteria, some of which have taken up to four years to devise, it inhibits the creation of new examination titles. It also discourages development in areas of the curriculum that do not conform easily to existing subjects and schemes; like integrated studies, for example. Lastly, by subjecting schools and departments to a list of national criteria, it gives little scope for the development of new curriculum-related assessment initiatives at school level. It undermines school based curriculum development and school based examining of the earlier 'Mode 3' type (Torrance, 1985, 1987).

In short, because of its employment of national criteria, the GCSE will restrict curricular breadth, undermine school based development and change, and stifle individual teacher initiative. It will encourage narrowing and ossification of the curriculum in a way that will be prejudicial to socialist and social democratic interests. Nor will this necessarily be offset by changes in teaching style. For we have seen that while national criteria might limit the content that teachers can cover, their potential to reshape teachers' long-standing approaches to their teaching is not sufficiently great to penetrate the autonomy of the classroom. The persistence of public examinations at 16, the requirement that schools publish their results, and the consequent rating of schools and teachers by their examination record is not going to do much for encouraging more 'high risk', open-ended strategies of teaching either. Nor, given that independence, initiative and involvement have been taken away from teachers by the national criteria, is it likely that teachers will have the motivation and commitment to change their styles in the way GCSE requires. Taking all these things together, it is therefore clear that an effective socialist educational policy must involve a re-evaluation of the GCSE and of the principle of public examinations at 16 as a whole.

Graded Tests and Assessments

The development of graded tests and assessments, from their experimental application in a limited number of school subjects like music and modern languages, to their incorporation, in one way or another, into broad schemes of 'Records of Achievement' constitutes one of the most significant developments in educational assessment in recent years. Such 'Records of Achievement' are now used in the ILEA, in the West Midlands, among the 22 Local Education Authorities (LEAs) who are members of the 'Northern Partnership', and within the Oxford Certificate of Educational Achievement, for instance.

The advantages of such schemes of graded assessment and testing, it is claimed, are; that they set short, achievable targets which pupils can work towards with a realistic sense of purpose in a way that they find difficult during the conventional two-year haul of narrow examination based courses; they enable virtually all students to have their achievements recognized (however modest); they encourage individualization of the learning process through the principle that pupils be tested and assessed not *en masse* but only when they are personally ready; and by setting new criteria of achievement (for instance in practical or oral work), they encourage changes in teaching method (Harrison, 1982; HMI, 1983; Murphy and Pennycuick, 1987).

A system of assessment geared to continuous work, in an individualized way, such that it is integrated closely into the fabric of the curriculum might, in principle, enhance and improve the learning process more than the one-off examination (although it should be remembered that graded assessments are a complement to the public examination system, not a substitute for it). There are, however, a number of key issues in this area about which the Left might have legitimate cause for concern.

Examination issues giving cause for concern
First, despite an elaborate rhetoric of justification, the essential impetus behind graded assessments may amount to little more than acceptance of the principle that 'pupils like to receive certificates' – as HMI concluded in a recent survey of one LEA's use of graded tests in modern languages (HMI, 1985). Initially, this may perhaps be true. But one wonders whether over time, pupils will become aware that these graded certificates are not spurring them on to higher levels of achievement, but, at the lower levels at least, are simply acknowledging what they can already do. Within the development of graded assessment schemes, the lower levels of achievement are indeed specified on the basis of surveys of existing pupil competence which show that most pupils have, at the expected age, already mastered the relevant skill and concepts (GAIM, 1986). Of course, giving recognition to a pupil's existing

success may still be educationally worthwhile. But this is a very different matter from actually *raising* standards of achievement.

Secondly, many good things in education are effective because they are exceptions; a bit different from the mainstream. The danger is that sometimes onlookers can become so impressed by these new initiatives that they feel tempted to spread them across the rest of the curriculum. As soon as this happens, though, they lose their special value. They suffer from overkill and become as ordinary and routine as the systems they replaced. Awarding certificates for graded tests, one suspects, is prone to this danger. Where they are rare, hard to earn, and only to be found in some parts of the curriculum, certificates are like gold sovereigns: their currency value is high. When they are easily earned and can be collected anywhere, the certificates become more like Spanish pesetas: their currency is devalued. People are no longer specially motivated to collect them. One suspects, then, that the motivating force of graded tests, when used across the curriculum, will turn out to be much more limited than enthusiasts in particular subjects have claimed.

Thirdly, the concentration on short-term targets, with its appeal to pupils' extrinsic motivation, may shorten the otherwise dauntingly distant horizons of educational success. But in shortening those horizons, might graded tests/assessments not also limit them? Will it encourage young people to run from one modular skyline to the next without ever having grasped the nature and purpose of the course as a whole? One of the dangers, in directing learning to such short-term targets, is that pupils and teachers may be wholly motivated towards acquiring the course certificate at the expense of being concerned about the intrinsic purpose and validity of what is being taught and learned. Another problem is that when graded assessments are linked to principles of credit accumulation for successful completion of short units or modules of study, pupils may become bewildered by the system of coherence and interrelationship between the credits and modules as a whole, and may find it difficult to assess the implications of all this for their wider educational and social opportunities. That is, in shortening horizons, graded tests and assessments may contribute to a confusion and mystification about educational choice and its implications for life and work after school, which is far greater than the much criticized, more conventional system of option choice at 14 (Ball, 1981; Woods, 1979). Pupils, with their educational horizons now foreshortened, might be more easily open to 'guidance' – manipulation and channelling – and to covert selection by their teachers who have a greater and deeper but also more inaccessible and unchallengeable knowledge of the curriculum as a whole.

Lastly, with the GCSE, teachers and pupils involved in graded assessment schemes may become increasingly subject to what Apple (1982) calls the logic of technical control – the subservience of their curriculum and learning needs to closely specified criteria drawn up at national and regional level. Witness all the professional effort expended in writing purportedly unambiguous/ non-jargonized 'descriptors' at each level (Sutton, 1986). Such systems of curriculum control might help bring about initial curriculum change. But once instituted, these descriptions and criteria run the risk of de-skilling the teacher, of undermining his or her own professional judgement; in addition to inhibiting possibilities for further change and development.

A fourth concern is that graded assessments have predominantly been developed within existing, conventional subject areas – most usually the high status ones of mathematics, science, modern languages and English – though increasingly craft, design and technology (CDT) as well. This development of graded assessment within existing high status subject areas of the secondary curriculum is unfortunate and has been much criticized – in response to the Schools Council sponsored 'Manchester Assessment Project' for instance (Sutton, 1986). The development of graded assessments within certain subjects only endorses and reinforces the untoward importance these subjects are already accorded in comparison with other areas of the curriculum. It endorses and reinforces the existing division of the curriculum on subject specialist lines. It inhibits the development of assessment policies on a cross-curricular basis (or by implication deems these to be of lower importance than the skills developed within 'real subjects'). And it makes it even harder for new, emergent and currently marginalized areas of the curriculum, such as environmental education, world studies, political education and the like, to gain coverage, status and recognition in the curriculum on a par with the more traditional specialisms.

A fifth examination issue is that as presently defined, subject based graded assessments could well end up 'conning' pupils into believing they have gained special achievements (when they might well have done so anyway). The assessment grades are prone to devaluation as their use spreads across the curriculum. They run the risk of reducing pupils' involvement in and grasp of the overall purpose and coherence of the parts of the curriculum they are studying and, indeed, the coherence of the modular or credit based curriculum structure as a whole, with all the implications this has for their own educational and social opportunities. They run the risk of buttressing the already well established priorities accorded to conventional subject specialisms in the secondary curriculum, at the expense of emergent and currently marginalized areas whose purpose is to explore those areas of human concern and controversy, a consideration of which is or should be such a vital part of the socialist educational agenda. And, unless their relationship to the GCSE is clearly defined on a basis that recognizes equivalence of status between them, they are in danger of being outflanked by the preoccupations with public examinations.

It seems to me, therefore, that the Left, needs to consider its position in relation to subject based graded assessments and associated schemes of accumulated course credits very carefully indeed; since they can easily lead to narrowing of the curriculum, shortening of pupils' horizons, and to opening pupils up to covert, non-accountable processes of selection and differentiation through modular and credit based systems – especially among those likely to be designated as 'less able'.

Pupil Profiles and Records of Achievement

The expansion of pupil profiles and records of achievement from a point of relative obscurity in the early 1980s when apparently fewer than 1 per cent of all secondary schools used them (Balogh, 1983); to a situation where universal adoption in all state secondary schools is expected by the end of the decade (DES, 1984), is a remarkably rapid educational development, even by modern standards. Many reasons have been put forward in support of their development, not least by the DES (1984) itself. These include:

– The recognition of alternative kinds of educational achievement (especially social and personal achievement) among the young, to the ones normally rewarded through public examinations.

– The increasing prominence (because of this recognition) that profiles and records of achievement will give to these alternative forms of achievement within the curriculum.

– The enhancement of pupil motivation (especially in circumstances of growing youth unemployment) within schools, as non-academic achievements and experiences are given greater emphasis and recognition in the curriculum.

– The involvement of pupils in their own assessment (self-assessment) and hence, the development in them of greater responsibility for their own learning.

– The development of more effective procedures for diagnosing learning needs and difficulties.

– Democratization of the teacher-pupil relationship resulting from the processes of negotiation and discussion involved in profile assessment.

– Curriculum change, as pupils are increasingly involved in negotiations about curriculum, and teachers are given systematic and repeated feedback on the impact and effectiveness of what they teach and how they teach it.

– Its comprehensive availability as a matter of entitlement to pupils of all ages and abilities, not just the less able.

From a socialist point of view, profiles and records of achievement have the potential to give status to achievements outside the academic domain: to increase pupils' independence, assertiveness and critical judgement; to involve young people more in their own education; to humanize the teacher-pupil relationship; and to give pupils a greater say in the curriculum they learn in. For socialists, of course, there remain all the usual important questions about the need to provide adequate time, staffing and resources to enable this pattern of personalized assessment to be carried out effectively. But there are more fundamental questions to be resolved, also concerning the overall purposes of profiling, the very different uses to which profiles and records of personal achievement can be put, and the threat this can pose to the purposes of independence and collaboration that many have invested in the profile innovation. Not everyone sees profiles as vehicles for radical change and personal liberation, as the Junior Education Minister, Bob Dunn has himself hinted by issuing the following warning.

'If we are to achieve consensus we must be realistic. Pilot work on existing new initiatives naturally attracts enthusiasts.' [That classically understated term of upper class abuse! – AH]. 'This is exactly as it should be. Some even see records of achievement as the herald of an educational revolution in the classroom. Perhaps this may prove to be so in the long term. But *we must not allow ourselves to be carried away*' (author's emphasis)

(Dunn, 1986: 5).

I have discussed the conflicts of purpose and difficulties involved in records of achievement in some detail elsewhere. (A. Hargreaves,

1985, 1986b; Hargreaves *et al*, 1987) and so shall review them only briefly here.

Conflicts of purpose and difficulties

One of the major aims behind the development of profiles and records of achievement, at least for the DES, is that they should ultimately lead to a document which can be presented to employers or other 'users'. In other words, many of those involved in profiles still hope that they will contribute to occupational *selection*. One of the difficulties of profiles being used for these purposes, and not just for the pupils alone, is that the ultimate knowledge that profiles will be used for selection purposes (even if only with the young person's permission) may have a backwash effect on the continuing formative processes of discussion and negotiation between teacher and pupil. Will the more unusual students – the rastafarians, the animal rights campaigners, the feminists etc, – declare their identity and interests at the risk of prejudicing how these things might be perceived by an employer or other external 'user'? Or, will they develop the strategic capacity to declare what they are not, for the benefit of those users and to increase, perhaps, their occupational marketability, at the expense of their own personal integrity?

There are various ways of managing these sorts of dilemmas; not least by making a strict separation between the long formative process of discussion and negotiation over a young person's educational career, and the calculated construction of a final document (with an eye on the likely perceptions of employers and other external users). But one wonders also how far, in the present context of widespread youth unemployment, employers need to be involved in the design, development and use of records of personal achievement at all? Would it not now be expedient to remove them from involvement in pupil profiles, given that their role as receivers of 16-year-olds is already becoming redundant? In many respects, it is arguable that employers have often been involved in the business of profile development, less for reasons of their own practical need, than out of schools' educational deference (under implied political pressure) to dominant industrial values. Under a socialist government, there is no reason why this kind of gratuitous vocationalism need continue.

Secondly, profiles can be used to enhance independence, but they can also be used as instruments of social control: as ways of securing conformity to the system, of heading off deviance before it starts, of prying into and keeping track of emotions and feelings that might have disruptive consequences for the school. In this respect, one needs to ask whether the agenda for any one-to-one discussion is framed to serve the pupil's interests or the school's. Questions like the one that appears in the profile used by one LEA (Warwickshire) for instance – 'I believe it is important to keep up the reputation of the school – YES/NO' – clearly serve the interests of the latter. Overemphasis on matters of appearance, timekeeping, remembering homework etc, is also a sign that teachers are trying to serve their own control interests instead of the personal needs of their pupils. The establishment of learning contracts, of agreed targets for the future, which show statements of intended behavioural change on the part of the pupils, but few similar such undertakings on the part of the teacher, also indicates that profiling is being used as a one-sided mechanism for imposing control, and not a two-sided, open-ended process of discussion and negotiation in a learning partnership.

Where profiles and personal record-keeping are open to these kinds of abuse, procedures for storing and gaining access to recorded information which the pupil might regard as private and confidential, or personally sensitive, will need to be carefully drawn up and scrupulously checked – especially where such storage is computerized. Who will have access to pupils' personally compiled records? Will the pastoral care system be able to plug into it anytime it has a problem to solve? Or, will pupils be able to exercise veto over access to all or parts of their continuous statements? Socialists and social democrats alike will need to think carefully about the ways in which such individual freedoms can be protected, and the storage of sensitive personal data regulated. This is important not only to protect human dignity, but in order to make the process meaningful. There is evidence to suggest that where pupils do feel evidence may be used against them, where they feel that other adults have a too easy access to what they record, where they feel that their records can become the subject of gossip among teachers and their colleagues – where, in other words, they feel they cannot trust their teachers to keep confidences – then they will not record anything of value in the first place (Hargreaves *et al*, 1987). In these circumstances, the profiling process can rapidly degenerate into a dreary routine for teachers and pupils alike.

One vital issue for those concerned about the need to protect personal privacy, is the extent to which records of achievement encompass home and family life, as well as achievements at school. It is probably right that young people be given the opportunity to bring their achievements out of school to the attention of their teachers, so that they might develop more positive conceptions of those young people's capabilities. It is probably also advisable to draw parents into the learning partnership with teachers and pupils, discussing and contributing to what their children have achieved and can achieve (ILEA, 1985). But when, as in the Warwickshire profile, parents are asked to comment on and indeed *assess* their children's performance in the family – to assess how well they keep their bike in repair, if they can be trusted on it, how often they do the vacuuming, how they handle their pocket money, and how good they are at getting up in the morning – something else is happening as well as involving parents in the learning partnership. The state, in fact, is extending its influence and surveillance into areas of people's private lives over which it should have no proper jurisdiction. It is asking parents to spy on their children's personal habits and, by implication, assessing those parents and the quality of their home lives too, according to a yardstick of middle-class manners and morality. Socialists and social democrats ought to address themselves to such unwarranted extensions of state influence into the private and domestic spheres.

To sum up: profiles and records of achievement can be particularly helpful in some of the more marginalized areas of the curriculum with which this book is concerned – by deepening pupils' involvement in the curriculum, heightening their critical awareness, and so on – without converting the study of contemporary human affairs into just another examined academic subject. But profiles and records of achievement can be used as techniques of surveillance and selection as well. Socialists and social democrats need to think through how profiles might usefully be turned to the first set of purposes, and prevented from encompassing and being dominated by the second. Commitment and clarification of purpose will be important priorities here. So too will the provision of adequate time and resources to allow profiles to develop in a more flexible, pupil-centred way. And the shadow that the GCSE casts over parallel developments, like records of achievement, putting them in the shadow of its own high profile, will warrant attention also.

Conclusion

Clearly, assessment involves much more than selection. It is a central part and determinant of the learning process, not just its culmination. Conservatives have shrewdly grasped the educational importance of assessment and made it a central and compelling feature of their policy. Socialists concerned with educational policy-making would do well to do likewise, by placing assessment high on its list of policy priorities *now*, and not simply deferring its discussion to a future and distant Educational Council. Much of the important professional detail would, of course, be left to such a Council, but its work might best be conducted within a confidently stated set of broad political guidelines. Principles that such guidelines might affirm, could include the following:

– Minimizing the role of assessment in relation to educational selection.

– Delaying the use of educational assessment in relation to selection until as late a point as possible in a young person's career – and certainly beyond 16.

– Giving very serious consideration to the abolition of the GCSE.

– Extending the process of education and training for all beyond 16 to 17 and then 18, with possible retention of public examination at these later stages for those considering entry to higher education (though that principle too might be reviewed in due course).

– Reintegrating policies on assessment with ones on an agreed, broad and balanced range of curriculum content, so that assessment is made a firm and integral part of socialist education policy on comprehensive curricular entitlement.

– Allowing any common curriculum to be divided into easily digestible chunks or modular components where appropriate, but guarding against modular systems being used as disguised and non-accountable forms of option choice, with all its selective implications.

– Assessing performance until 16 on a continuous, not a one-off basis, through graded assessments and pupil profiles.

– Allowing high local flexibility in the development of graded assessments and profiles within broad guidelines, to increase teachers' ownership of and therefore commitment to them. Regional consortia of examination boards, LEAs and teachers might well take on this kind of work.

– Checking that graded assessments do not degenerate into the large-scale production of certificates, but that they award these judiciously, where real achievements have been made.

– Ensuring that graded assessment schemes maintain an

emphasis on improving the quality of the learning process and the forms of intrinsic motivation that come with that, more than on merely awarding certificates in order to create extrinsic motivation.

– Removing employers from involvement in records of achievement in order to eradicate the gratuitous vocationalism that creeps into the recording process.

– Establishing clear procedures for access to pupil data compiled through the recording process in order to protect privacy and confidentiality. This might include 'coding' data (by the pupil, and under his or her control) at different levels of confidentiality, each of which entails progressively wider access.

– Setting up a 'National Accrediting Body' for records of achievement whose principles would include ensuring that such records do not infringe the privacy or personal liberty of the pupil, that they do not involve employers unless they would be direct users of any such records, and that they are not designed as mechanisms of behavioural control but as tools of personal development.

References

Apple, M. (1982) *Education & Power*. Routledge & Kegan Paul, London.

Baglin, E. (1984) *A case study of a social education department*. Dissertation for the Special Diploma in Educational Studies. Department of Education, University of Oxford.

Ball, S. (1981) *Beachside Comprehensive*. Cambridge University Press.

Balogh, J. (1983) *Profile Reports for School Leavers*. Longmans, York.

Broadfoot, P. (1979) *Assessment, Schools and Society*, Methuen, London.

Broadfoot, P. (1984) 'From public examinations to profile assessment: the French experience'. In Broadfoot, P. (ed) *Selection, Certification and Control*. Falmer Press, Lewes.

Broadfoot, P. (1986) 'Assessment Policy and Inequality: the United Kingdom experience'. *British Journal of Sociology of Education*, 7 (2).

Burgess, R. (1984) 'It's not a proper subject: it's just Newsom'. Goodson, I. and Ball, S. In *Defining the Curriculum*. Falmer Press, Lewes.

Centre for Contemporary Cultural Studies (CCCS) (1981) *Unpopular Education* Hutchinson, London.

Cox, C. & Scruton, R. (1984) *Peace Studies: a Critical Survey*. Occasional Paper No 7, Institute for European Defence and Strategic Studies. Alliance Publishers, London.

Denscombe, M. (1985) *Classroom Control: a sociological perspective*, Allen & Unwin, London.

Department of Education & Science (1984) *Records of Achievement: a statement of policy*. HMSO, London.

Dunn, R. (1986) Speech to the London Education Business Partnership, 11th November.

Evans, J. (1985) *Teaching in Transition*. Open University Press, Milton Keynes.

Goodson, I. (1983) 'Subjects for Study: aspects of a social history of curriculum', *Journal of Curriculum Studies*, 15, (4).

Graded Assessments in Mathematics (GAIM) (1986) *Newsletter 4*, Spring Term.

Gray, J. McPherson, A.F. and Raffe, D. (1983) *Reconstructions of Secondary Education*, Routledge & Kegan Paul, London.

Hammersley, M. and Scarth, J. (1986) *The Impact of Examinations in Secondary School Teaching: a research report*. Unpublished, November, School of Education, Open University.

Hargreaves, A. (1985) 'Motivation versus Selection: some dilemmas for records of personal achievement' in Lang, P. & Marland, M. *New Directions in Pastoral Care*, Basil Blackwell, Oxford.

Hargreaves, A. (1986a) *Two Cultures of Schooling: the case of middle schools*, Falmer Press, Lewes.

Hargreaves, A. (1986b) 'Recordbreakers?' In Broadfoot, P. (ed.) *Profiles & Records of Achievement*, Holt-Saunders, Eastbourne.

Hargreaves, A. (forthcoming) 'The Crisis of Motivation & Assessment'. In Hargreaves, and Reynolds, D. *Education Policy Initiatives; Controversies & Critiques*, Falmer Press, Lewes.

Hargreaves, A. (forthcoming) 'Teaching Quality: a sociological analysis', *Journal of Curriculum Studies*.

Hargreaves, A. *et al* (1987) *Social & Personal Education: Choices and Challenges*, Basil Blackwell, Oxford.

Hargreaves, D. (1982) *The Challenge for the Comprehensive School*, Routledge & Kegan Paul, London.

Harrison, A. (1982) *Review of Graded Tests*, Schools Council Examinations Bulletin 41. Methuen Educational, London.

Her Majesty's Inspectorate (1979) *Aspects of Secondary Education*. HMSO, London.

Her Majesty's Inspectorate (1983) A survey of the use of graded tests of defined objectives and their effect on teaching and learning in modern languages in the County of Oxfordshire.

Her Majesty's Inspectorate (1985) 'Report by HM Inspectors on a survey of work in modern languages in 27 schools in the Leeds Metropolitan District taking graded tests of defined objectives in modern languages'.

Hitchcock, G. (1986) *Profiles & Profiling*. Longman, Harlow.

ILEA (1984) *Improving Secondary Schools*. ILEA, London.

ILEA (1985) *Profiling in ILEA Secondary Schools*. ILEA, London.

Murphy, R. and Pennycuick, D. (1987) 'Graded Assessments and the GCSE'. In Horton, T. (ed.) *GCSE: examining the new system* Harper & Row, London.

Nuttall, D. (1984) 'Doomsday or a new dawn: the prospects for a common system of examining at 16+'. In Broadfoot, P. (ed.), *Selection, Certification and Control*. Falmer Press, Lewes.

Olson, J. (1982) *Innovation in the Science Curriculum*, Croom Helm, London.

Radice, G. (1986) *Equality and Quality: A Socialist Plan for Education*. Fabian Society Pamphlet no. 514. Fabian Society, London.

Ranson, S. & Tomlinson J. (eds.) (1986) *The Changing Government of Education*. Allen & Unwin, London.

Riseborough, G. (1981) 'Teacher Careers & Comprehensive Schooling'. *Sociology* 15 (3) pp. 355-381.

Roy, W. (1987) 'The Teacher Viewpoint'. In Horton, T. (ed.) *GCSE – Examining The New System*. Harper & Row, London.

Salter, B. & Tapper, T. (1987) *Department of Education – steering a new course*. In Horton, T. (ed.). GCSE – *Examining the New System*, Harper & Row, London.

Scarth, J. (1983) 'Teachers' school-based experiences of examining'. In Hammersley, M. and Hargreaves A. *Curriculum Practice: some sociological case studies*. Falmer Press, Lewes.

Scarth, J. (1987) 'Teaching to the Exam? – the case of the Schools Council History Project'. In Horton, T. (ed.) *GCSE: Examining the New System*, Harper and Row, London.

Scarth, J. & Hammersley, M. (1986) 'Examinations and teaching; an exploratory study'. Unpublished mimec.

Scruton, R. Ellis Jones, A. and O'Keefe, D. (1985) *Education and Indoctrination*. Sherwood Press, London.

Sikes, P. Measor, L. & Woods, P. (1985) *Teachers' Careers*. Falmer Press, Lewes.

Simon, B. (1985) *Does Education Matter?* Lawrence and Wishart, London.

Socialist Education Association (1986) *Better Schools*. Socialist Education Association, London.

Sutton, R. (1986) *Assessment in Secondary Schools: the Manchester experience*. Longmans, York.

Torrance, H. (1985) 'Current Prospects for School Based Examining'. *Educational Review*, 371 (1) pp. 39-51.

Torrance, H. (1987) 'GCSE and School Based Curriculum Development'. In Horton, T. (ed.); *GCSE: examining the new system*. Harper & Row, London.

Tye, B. (1985) *Multiple Realities: a study of 13 American High Schools*. University Press of America, London.

Weston, P. (1979) *Negotiating the Curriculum*, NFER, Windsor.

Whitty, G. (1985) *Sociology and School Knowledge*. Methuen, London.

Woods, P. (1979) *The Divided School*. Routledge and Kegan Paul, London.

Woods, P. (forthcoming) 'Ethnography at the Crossroads: a reply to Hammersley', *British Educational Research Journal*.

Chapter 2.3

INTEGRATED HUMANITIES: A CURRICULUM CONTEXT FOR ECOLOGY AND DEVELOPMENT EDUCATION?

Geoff Whitty,
Bristol Polytechnic

One of the organizers of the recent conference on 'Education, Ecology and Development' has suggested that the response of the educational system to the major problems that exist on a world and national scale in the field of ecology and development has been to marginalize and technologize them. It is difficult to quarrel with this view. It is also true that such issues are only beginning to find their way into schools on the fringes of biology and geography and through projects of the kind funded by the World Wildlife Fund and other organizations. However, a few schools have made the exploration of such issues a more major feature of their curricula for many years, even at examination level, by the introduction of integrated and inter-disciplinary humanities courses. Although these courses have enabled such issues to be explored in a way that avoids technologizing them, they have themselves often been marginalized within the educational system as a whole. Nevertheless, I want to argue in this paper that a number of contemporary developments make such courses increasingly attractive to schools, hence becoming a potential context within which the issues of most concern to us can begin to move on to the mainstream educational agenda. This is not to deny the role of other innovative curricular contexts, such as integrated science or world studies, in this process, but to argue that integrated humanities is a particularly apposite vehicle for our work at this point in time. This applies not only to the issues with which we are directly concerned today, but also to others which might form the focus of future concern.

It is important to stress from the outset that integrated humanities is not synonymous with terms like 'socialist education' or even with a 'socialist approach to education'; but it is a context within which work informed by what might broadly be termed socialist ideals is more likely to flourish than within many other curricular structures. This is partly because integrated humanities is centrally concerned with an exploration of the human condition and partly because, being less hidebound by tradition than conventional curricular subjects, both its content and its pedagogic form tend to be 'negotiable'. This does not mean that it is a field that can simply be colonized by socialist educators, but it is a field in which contestation of the terrain has already brought about important gains in some schools. I have recently argued (Whitty, 1985) that a recognition that we are unlikely to establish an entirely socialist approach to education within the educational institutions of a capitalist state, has too often been taken as a reason either to accept an unsatisfactory *status quo* or to regard reactionary trends as inevitable. However, because the curriculum is always produced by compromises between different interest groups (Williams, 1961), it is important to mobilize our own preferred alternatives to produce different compromises than would otherwise exist without our intervention. My argument is that integrated humanities is a context within which we might push that compromise just that little bit further in a direction that is consistent with our broader political objectives.

In this paper, I shall draw largely upon my own experience, as a teacher of humanities (at Thomas Bennett School in Crawley), as a trainer of humanities teachers (at Bath University) and, more recently, as chair of the 'Humanities Subject Working Party' of the Southern Examining Group and Moderator for two Mode 3 Humanities courses for the University of London School Examinations Board, one of which has been developed as part of a TVEI curriculum. I hope that this approach will help to encourage the sharing of experience among readers and a full and frank evaluation of my claim that integrated humanities is currently one of the more hopeful contexts for the sort of meaningful and critical education which we are seeking to develop. I use the term integrated humanities here, with some reservations, in the generic sense now apparently being employed by the GCSE examining groups to cover integrated, combined, inter-disciplinary and multi-disciplinary humanities courses.

My own early experience in the humanities field is described in greater detail in *Developments in Social Studies Teaching* (Gleeson and Whitty, 1976). There we chart the history of humanities teaching in the late sixties and early seventies, a period which saw a number of worthy efforts to scrutinize and rethink the nature of education in the humanities field. The main styles of humanities teaching were characterized there as follows:

Model 1: **Single Disciplinary Study**
    (a) transmission of subject knowledge
    (b) initiation into subject methodology

Model 2: **Structured Inter-disciplinary Enquiry**
    (a) broad themes of 'enduring human concern'
    (b) initiation into a 'mode of enquiry', using subjects
        as tools

Model 3: **Free-Ranging Enquiry**
    (a) pupil-initiated enquiry with teacher as facilitator
        of learning
    (b) collaborative enquiry

We suggested that, although the vast majority of schools still operated within Model 1 (and probably Model 1(a) at that), some schools were beginning to re-examine the whole notion of teaching the humanities as separate academic subjects, especially for lower school and lower band pupils. Moreover, in a few schools, such as the three whose work was discussed in the book, this had extended to a questioning of the appropriateness of Model 1 for pupils of all abilities and it had even embraced courses leading to external examinations at 16+.

This rethinking of the nature of humanities teaching had led to the introduction of various kinds of integrated, interdisciplinary and multi-disciplinary humanities courses. These new courses were often concerned to use the resources of the various humanities disciplines to study broad themes either of 'enduring human concern' or of supposed 'relevance' to the pupils' present or future lives outside school. Themes like conflict, conservation, the family, leisure, etc, were commonplace within such courses. In some cases, the new syllabuses had merely involved the rearrangement of existing subject matter and they brought about little change in prevailing styles of pedagogy. In other cases, there had been a deliberate attempt to place the major emphasis on fostering enquiry skills in recognition of the argument that the so-called 'knowledge explosion' was rendering knowledge of subject matter much less valuable than knowledge of ways of finding out. A very few schools were, at that time, going even further and moving into Model 3, in which there was no pre-defined syllabus in the accepted sense, and in which the role of the teacher was to facilitate whatever enquiries pupils wished to initiate.

The three courses described in our book (at Thomas Bennett

School, at Dorcan School in Swindon and at Hartcliffe School in Bristol) were all centrally located within Model 2, though two of them (Thomas Bennett and Dorcan) retained some elements of Model 1, and two of them (Thomas Bennett and Hartcliffe) undertook modest experiments in the spirit of Model 3. In the case of Thomas Bennett School, the humanities programme in the fourth and fifth years replaced all other humanities teaching in those years, while Hartcliffe retained a range of options alongside the humanities core and Dorcan permitted some candidates to take additional subjects.

The contexts within which such courses were introduced varied considerably from school to school. In some cases, they were part of wider attempts to introduce a common core curriculum, while in others they were *ad hoc* experiments. The former approach was most typical in new schools. Of the courses discussed in the *Developments in Social Studies Teaching*, that at Dorcan School, like the more widely known courses at Sheredes School in Hertfordshire and at various schools and community colleges in Leicestershire, had the advantage of being introduced in a new school where curriculum thinking could start with a clean sheet. Those at Thomas Bennett School and Hartcliffe School were introduced by making drastic changes to pre-existing curricular arrangements and were perhaps a better test of the extent to which such innovations could be generalized.

The Thomas Bennett examination syllabus combined many of the elements which were typical of these courses and it is reproduced here as it appeared in the early seventies:

Historical and Social Studies	Geographical and Community Studies
Fourth Year (Discipline-based themes)	
– Industrialization and society	– Socialization and the family
– The coming of the welfare state	– Land use and regional studies
– The British economy today	– Urban studies
Fifth Year (Issue-based themes)	
– Race relations	– Education and social divisions
– War	– Underdevelopment and aid
– International relations	– Pollution and conservation

The course was given timetable space equivalent to that for two conventional subjects and pupils were thus able to study each theme in considerable depth for periods of up to a term. At the end of the courses, pupils were entered for Mode 3 O levels or CSEs in Historical and Social Studies and/or Geographical and Community Studies.

Despite having many criticisms of the course, some of which are rehearsed in the book (Gleeson and Whitty, 1976) my experience of this course (and later of those at Dorcan and Hartcliffe) was broadly a positive one. I was certainly convinced that such courses made it far more possible to bring pupils to engage meaningfully and critically with issues of social concern than the history and social studies courses which I had taught hitherto. For a short time, it looked as if such humanities courses might spread quite rapidly, even at examination level, as other teachers began to see in them the opportunity to introduce more flexible curricula and get away from the sterility and perceived irrelevance of more typical humanities subjects (Schools Council, 1968). In the mid-1970s, like other teachers who had been involved in such programmes, I received many invitations to talk to in-service courses about the attractions of the approach.

However, in the late seventies, such invitations began to dry up and the enthusiasm for innovations of this sort waned. Though those that had been well established in the first three years of secondary schools usually survived, as did those for 'less able' pupils, they did not spread as rapidly as we had envisaged to examination courses, especially at O level. This made it difficult for integrated humanities to achieve a comparable status with more conventional school subjects (Goodson, 1983). Indeed, some of the existing fourth and fifth year humanities programmes were abandoned or curtailed, as was the case at Thomas Bennett itself, where the core provision was eventually reduced and single subject humanities options reintroduced alongside it.

The reasons for this decline of enthusiasm for broadly based humanities programmes were varied, some resulting from deficiencies of the programmes themselves, some to do with the general climate within schools and examination boards at that time, and others a reflection of the extent to which the individual humanities subjects had reformed themselves in response to what they perceived as a threat. For example, some of the Schools Council projects in history and geography reflected almost as great a concern with enquiry skills and relevance as did some of the early humanities programmes, even though their scope was narrower.

However, in 1981-82, when my own interests had actually developed away from humanities teaching, (except in my role as Moderator of a surviving Mode 3 O level course at Hextable School in Kent), I began once again to receive invitations to participate in in-service courses on the subject of integrated humanities. In addition, I was asked by Henry Macintosh to convene a panel of interested parties, on behalf of the Future Curriculum Trends Working Party of the recently established Southern Examining Group, to consider the need for a broadly based humanities course within the new 16+ examination. When the panel presented its initial report, advocating the inclusion of humanities as an examination subject in the Group's offerings at 16+, there was considerable scepticism on the part of some members of the Group's senior committees about both the necessity and the desirability of making such provision. There was even more criticism about some of the more radical features of our proposal, and on some of these issues, such as whether to include a terminal examination, we felt it politic to compromise. It was only this, together with Henry Macintosh's steadfast determination to force the Group to look to the future, that kept our panel in existence throughout four long years of negotiations.

However, by the time our final proposals were accepted in June 1986, we were able to take advantage of a climate that had changed substantially. There was a general recognition in the Group that it desperately needed an integrated humanities syllabus, if it was to meet the needs of schools in 1990s. Indeed, towards the end of our deliberations we were positively encouraged to reinstate some of the more radical elements of the proposal (such as 100 per cent school based assessment within a Mode 1 syllabus) to give schools that very flexibility which, in the early days, had been seen not only as unnecessary, but even as positively dangerous. To me this was a quite fascinating experience, having charted recently in *Sociology and School Knowledge* (Whitty, 1985) the ways in which the universities and GCE boards had imposed conventional models of syllabus development and assessment on the GCSE Groups in the early days of their existence. Here, though, was the reopening of the issues that I had predicted would take place once ministers and the industrial lobby recognized the extent to which the academic model of education had yet again prevailed, despite attempts in the 'Great Debate' and its aftermath to enhance the status of prevocational approaches to education. Here too was the opportunity for the left to exploit the differences between the old humanists and the industrial trainers to shift the curriculum compromise firmly in the direction of the public educators (William, 1961). To a limited degree, we had already tried to do this with the integrated humanities proposal, by demonstrating that the choice between 'rigour' and 'relevance' was an unnecessary one and thus gaining support for our syllabus from among both the other factions.

The proposal which has now been accepted by the Southern Examining Group is one of three which are now available (from September 1987) to GCSE candidates in England. The other two have been developed by the Midlands Examining Group and the Northern Examinations Association. The schemes differ in a number of respects, but also have common features. I shall concentrate here on the Southern Examining Group's syllabus, because it is the one I know best. The broad aims embraced by the syllabus include:

> 'an understanding of human societies ... and the range of personal futures in a world of rapid technological and cultural change; an awareness of the meaning and diversity of human values ... and preparation for responsible participation in a multi-cultural society; social, economic and political literacy ... at individual, community, national and global levels; and active and collaborative involvement in the learning process'.

The full list of aims is included in the Appendix to this paper.

The syllabus is partly skills based; these skills covering understanding, enquiry, analysis and evaluation, and communication (further details of which are again given in the Appendix). Schools can propose their own subject matter and examples of acceptable themes, from which pupils need to study five for single certification, or ten for double certification; some of the topics included are:

Community and environment	People and work
Urbanization	Recreation and conservation
Peace and conflict	Beliefs and values
Environmental management	World interdependence
The impact of technology	Race and culture
Human rights	Unity and division

A fuller list is given in the Appendix, but teachers are free to propose quite different alternatives. However, far from this flexibility being a recipe for what I recently heard an LEA adviser call 'the sort of chaos and anarchy that has too often reigned in primary schools' – presumably the 'anything goes' approach which lacks any sense of structure or progression – the syllabus actually requires schools to demonstrate how they intend to structure their subject matter in terms of certain *key concepts* and *key contexts*. These are as follows:

Required Contextual Levels	Required Conceptual Areas
Individual	Power and distribution
Community and local environment	Ideas and ideologies
National	Spatial interaction
Global and international	Continuity and change

Ironically, the same adviser who spoke of chaos and anarchy in primary schools, suggested to me that one of the problems of humanities syllabuses was that they permitted schools to avoid confronting pupils with world resource issues. It will be seen, however, that the combination of required concepts and contexts in this particular syllabus makes it far more likely that pupils will have to confront such issues within their humanities course than within many single-subject syllabuses. They are almost certain to have to confront global issues far more consistently and coherently than in most combinations of single-subject options. Furthermore, if integrated humanities becomes a core provision for all pupils, as our working party believes it ideally should be, such issues are far more likely to be confronted by pupils of all abilities.

What, then, apart from the fact that as chair of an integrated humanities subject panel I have a vested interest in its success, leads me to believe that this sort of syllabus has a bright future and that it will provide us with an appropriate context in which to carry out the sort of work in which we are interested today? What is it that makes me feel that the sceptical adviser quoted above may be somewhat out of step with current trends? First, I will outline some of the features of the present situation in schools that make such an approach more attractive than perhaps it was in the late seventies and which help to explain the recent conversion to the cause of integrated humanities by the Monitoring Committee of the Southern Examining Group. It will then be clear that, although it was certainly not a sudden espousal of socialism that led to their change of mind, this does not mean that socialist educators cannot take advantage of the situation that has now arisen.

The most obvious factor at work, of course, has been falling rolls, with the ensuing difficulties they present for schools trying to maintain a full range of curriculum subjects, especially where option choices are involved. However, alongside pressures for curriculum contraction, there have also been pressures for curriculum expansion, especially as governments and the public have placed new demands on schools. Although teachers of most individual subjects have been adept at arguing that their own subjects are ideally placed to meet all such demands (HMI, 1981), they can often be met far more coherently within core provision. The advantage of humanities providing that core is that it can treat these issues in a systematic rather than an *ad hoc* manner and it can combine a concern with social relevance with a commitment to academic rigour. Thus, for example, it can respond positively to demands that education should pay more attention to the world of work by encouraging pupils to explore actively the world outside school, but it can do so using the tools of critical analysis. For many teachers, this is preferable to the sort of low-status citizenship or social education course that merely inducts pupils uncritically into the labour market. Put simply, although in an ideal world many teachers of history or sociology might prefer to be left alone with their options, in the present situation, they would often prefer to develop one of the new style humanities courses than engage in the crude exercise in social control that some other courses involve.

Nevertheless, another innovation that critics often portray as a crude exercise in social control, the Technical and Vocational Education Initiative (TVEI) has itself given a recent boost to integrated humanities. Providing rather more flexibility than critics sometimes acknowledge, it has spawned integrated humanities courses where they did not exist before (including the Mode 3 course at Lea Manor High School in Luton where I act as O level Moderator). It was also TVEI schools and co-ordinators who were particularly vocal in persuading the Southern Examining Group to take our panel's proposals on integrated humanities seriously. Of course, their motives for wanting more flexible curriculum structures or more emphasis on experiential learning were by no means identical to our own. However, when there are also other progressive pressures working in the same direction, such as the proposals for modularized curricula contained in the Hargreaves Report (Hargreaves *et al*, 1984), socialist educators should not assume that such assaults on conventional curriculum arrangements need have wholly negative consequences. Rather, we should seize the opportunity they provide to shift the curriculum compromise in a direction that offers more to all pupils than either academic or pre-vocational curricula as currently conceived.

Another long-standing advocate of integrated humanities, Doug Holly, has recently acknowledged (Holly, 1986) that those who try to foster integrated humanities in a period of adversity might be accused of 'opportunism'. He prefers the term 'pragmatism', the difference being that, while opportunism makes use of circumstances to advance selfish ends, pragmatism reacts to circumstances by turning them to the general advantage. This 'positive reaction of principled realists' is what underlies the work of all the teachers who have contributed to Holly's volume and it is also, I hope, what will motivate the work of all those who read this book.

Appendix – GCSE Syllabus (Southern Examining Group)
Integrated Humanities
1988 Examination

Introduction
This syllabus conforms to the national general criteria for the GCSE. All GCSE grades are available on this syllabus.

The study of the humanities is in broad terms an exploration of the human condition. There are several methodologies and perspectives which can usefully be employed, and all the individual subject disciplines within the humanities may have a significant contribution to make towards this exploration. Humanities should, therefore, be seen as drawing upon *any* subject or aspect of a subject which contributes to the more rational or imaginative understanding of human situations.

In consequence, this integrated humanities syllabus has been designed as a skills framework, within which centres have the flexibility to determine the precise content and approaches to be adopted. Centres are required to select five topics (exemplars of which are given on page 144). The topic structure and the associated assessment pattern should lend the syllabus to modular applications.

The syllabus should, therefore, make it possible for centres to integrate and interrelate some of the methodologies and concepts of such disciplines as economics, geography, history, religious education, political studies, psychology and sociology in the consideration of broad themes and specific issues. Its broad based nature should provide a sound foundation for the specialist study of individual disciplines at Advanced Level. It should also be possible for courses based on the syllabus to draw upon elements of such subjects as craft, design and technology, personal relationships education, the expressive arts and the sciences.

The approach adopted emphasizes an enquiry based method of learning which is not confined by the boundaries of subject disciplines.

Aims
A course based on this syllabus should enable the following to be achieved:

1. An understanding of human societies which will enable informed and reasoned judgements to be made about significant contemporary issues.
2. An understanding of the social and cultural context of life in

modern society, and the range of possible personal futures in a world of rapid technological and cultural change.

3. An awareness of the meaning and diversity of human values, a sensitivity and empathy towards people living within different spatial, temporal, socio-economic and cultural contexts, and thus a preparation for responsible participation in a multi-cultural society.

4. Social, economic and political literacy, which will enable reasoned predictions to be made about the locus and likely consequences of decisions taken at individual, community, national and global levels.

5. Active and collaborative involvement in the learning process, which will enable candidates to develop decision-making skills and responsibility for the planning, direction and monitoring of their work.

These constitute general Aims for the course and cannot necessarily all be translated into Assessment Objectives.

Assessment objectives
The examination will assess a candidate's ability to:

1. *Understand* the disciplines, concepts and methods applicable to the topics being studied including:
   (a) the relevant disciplines;
   (b) the terminology involved in the study of the topics;
   (c) the main concepts used;
   (d) specific examples on which generalizations and concepts are based;
   (e) the sources of information which are available;
   (f) the methods of investigation which are available;
   (g) competing viewpoints and perspectives, demonstrating empathy with these;
   (h) the criteria for evaluation of evidence used.

2. *Enquire* critically and purposefully from a variety of information sources:
   (a) identify and discriminate between the possible sources of knowledge, both primary and secondary;
   (b) selectively use and interpret books, maps and numerical or quantitative material;
   (c) draw critically from experiences and encounters within the community;

(d) use resources outside the classroom – eg resource centres, libraries, museums, workplaces and external agencies;
(e) construct and conduct questionnaires and surveys;
(f) carry out other fieldwork – eg observation and recording;
(g) use imagination to develop hypotheses.

3. *Analyse and Evaluate* material:
(a) organize information;
(b) summarize findings;
(c) draw conclusions;
(d) test hypotheses;
(e) identify cause and effect;
(f) distinguish between fact and opinion, and detect bias;
(g) make ethical decisions relating to own personal life.

4. *Communicate* effectively in enquiry, analysis and presentation of material:
(a) use inter-personal and collaborative skills;
(b) demonstrate creativity;
(c) select and recognize appropriate techniques of presentation;
(d) demonstrate a range of writing styles;
(e) present information visually and numerically;
(f) demonstrate graphicacy.

Assessment pattern

All four sets of Syllabus Objectives are examined in each of three centre-assessed components according to the weightings shown in the 'Assessment objectives grid' on page 143.

The assessment pattern for the syllabus is common to all candidates, on the principle that the skills which humanities is seeking to promote can be achieved and demonstrated to some degree by all candidates, although clearly at different levels.

The use of three centre-assessed components will allow for a variety of tasks to be undertaken which differentiates between what the candidates know, understand and can do.

Paper 1: Assignments completed under Controlled Conditions – *30 per cent of the total marks*

For each of the five topics studied, candidates will be required to submit one assignment completed under controlled conditions, making five in all. Control is to be achieved through common elements of time, stimulus materials, approach to the task and degree of teacher guidance. Any stimulus material must be designed so as to be accessible to the full range of candidates' ability.

The relative weightings of the assessment objectives tested in Paper 1 are shown in the grid that follows on page 143.

Paper 2: Personal Research Study – *30 per cent of the total marks*

The Research Study will take the form of an investigation linked to a clearly formulated question or problem related to one of the topics studied. It should entail personal initiative and enquiry skills, and may be either theoretical or practical in its nature. The Research Study should enable evidence of individual work to be displayed, although it may be related to group activities.

The Personal Research Study should be designed to enable the assessment objectives of the syllabus to be tested in accordance with the weightings shown in the grid on page 143.

Candidates may complete the Research Study over any period of the course, and will present a folder of work for assessment and moderation at the end of the course.

Paper 3: Coursework – *40 per cent of the total marks*

Candidates will be required to submit four pieces of coursework, one drawn from each of four of the five topics studied.

The formulation and selection of coursework assignments should be negotiated between candidates and teachers. The assignments should be designed so that they:

(a) test the full range of cognitive skills and produce a discriminatory mark range;
(b) reflect a range of contextual levels from individual to global;
(c) reflect a range of conceptual ideas;
(d) test the assessment objectives in accordance with the weightings shown in the grid on page 143. It is recognized that each assignment may test a different balance of assessment objectives and that only across the four pieces must there be an equal balance between the four assessment objectives as specified.

Differentiation

Differentiation in the assignments completed under controlled conditions will be achieved by outcome. Centres will design common tasks accessible to the full ability range of their candidates. The marking guidelines will allow discrimination to be achieved on a positive basis over the complete range of ability.

Differentiation in the personal research study and coursework components will be achieved by the assigning of tasks to individual candidates according to the capabilities of each. The personal research study and the coursework components will be marked on common criteria for all candidates, with marks awarded to reflect the scope and difficulty of the tasks attempted and to discriminate across the complete ability range.

Relation between assessment pattern and assessment objectives
The assessment pattern is designed to ensure the use of techniques appropriate to the aims of the syllabus and the skills to be assessed.

In order to achieve a desirable balance between the various techniques of assessment and between the different sets of assessment objectives, centres are required to observe the distributions shown in the grid below.

Assessment Objectives Grid

Examination Component \ Objectives	Understanding	Enquiry	Analysis and evaluation	Communication	Total
Assignments completed under Controlled Conditions (Paper 1)	10	5	10	5	30
Personal research study (Paper 2)	5	10	5	10	30
Coursework (Paper 3)	10	10	10	10	40
Totals	25	25	25	25	100

Subject content
1.   Content is not specified too precisely because of the diversity of relevant subject matter, the changing significance of events and the desirability of students making appropriate use of resources and evidence from their own communities. However, the choice of the five substantive areas should be informed by the need to reflect the aims and assessment objectives above. Exemplars of topics from which centres may choose are given on page 144.

2.   To ensure that candidates' work
     (a) conforms to the aims of the syllabus, and
     (b) genuinely integrates or interrelates some of the methodologies and concepts of the humanities disciplines,
each centre is required to select five topics, each of which must be treated in such a way that the range of contextual levels and

conceptual areas described below is incorporated into the study.

Contextual Levels

The relationship of each chosen topic to:

(i) the *individual*;

(ii) the *community* and local environment;

(iii) the whole country or comparative studies within the country (the *national* scale);

(iv) the whole world or comparative studies between countries (the *global* or international scale).

Conceptual Areas

(i) *power* and distribution, ie the political dimension;

(ii) *ideas* and ideologies, ie the moral dimension;

(iii) spatial interaction (*space*), ie the geographical dimension;

(iv) continuity and *change*, ie the historical dimension.

3. The following list contains *examples* of the types of topic from which centres might choose, although alternatives may be submitted:

Community and environment	People and work
Urbanization	The family and child development
Industrialization	Recreation and conservation
Peace and conflict	Beliefs and values
Law and order	Marriage
Education	Health and welfare
Environmental management	Political movements
The impact of technology	Transport and communications
The mass media	World interdependence
Race and culture	Prejudice
Gender inequalities	Human rights
Unity and division	Wealth and poverty

4. Centres will be asked to demonstrate how their treatments of the topics chosen are to satisfy the requirements outlined above. It is important that across the five topics an equal balance be maintained within the four contextual and the four conceptual areas.

For each topic chosen, Centres are required to submit:

(i) a *topic matrix* indicating how that topic will be treated showing:

the weightings allocated to the four contextual levels and the four conceptual areas;

the ways in which the different contexts and concepts will be dealt with in the learning experience.

(ii)   a *topic statement*, in tabular form, about the proposed treatment describing:
key ideas;
learning activities;
resources;
nature of controlled assignment.

(The information in this appendix is reproduced with the permission of the Southern Examining Group.)

References

Gleeson, D. and Whitty, G. (1976) *Developments in Social Studies Teaching*. Open Books, London.

Goodson, I. (1983) *School Subjects and Curriculum Change*. Croom Helm, London.

HMI (1981) *Curriculum 11-16: a review of progress*. HMSO, London.

Holly, D. (ed) (1986) *Humanism in Adversity*. Falmer Press, Lewes.

Schools Council (1968) *Enquiry 1: Young School Leavers*. HMSO, London.

Whitty, G. (1985) *Sociology and School Knowledge: Curriculum Theory, Research and Practice*. Methuen, London.

Williams, R. (1961) *The Long Revolution*. Chatto and Windus, London.

Chapter 2.4

ENVIRONMENT AND DEVELOPMENT ISSUES IN THE CLASSROOM: THE EXPERIENCE OF ONE CURRICULUM PROJECT

John Huckle,
Bedford College of Higher Education

Fast food has become a staple of the young generation. It is sold in an environment where the decor, atmosphere, and uniforms are designed to stimulate excitement and advertised with images which promise everything nutritious, convenient and desirable. By 1985 McDonalds alone had a turnover of £11 billion a year and 165 branches in the UK. Yet few of the people who visit fast food outlets have any knowledge of the real costs of the food they buy. These include the resource costs of wasteful packaging, the costs clearing litter from the local streets and the costs paid by the low wage workers in such outlets who keep smiling despite the oppressive work methods. They also include the health costs associated with a diet high in sugar and additives and the costs paid by the producers of the food, often thousands of miles away. While the fast food chains have been anxious to deny their role in the destruction of tropical moist forests – some issuing law suits against well known environmentalists – there is evidence that beef from cattle grazed on the cleared areas is used by the fast food industry, particularly in North America. The real costs of fast food consumption may then include the costs of the climatic and ecological change associated with rainforest destruction and the costs of replacing the sustainable lifestyles of tribal peoples by something which favours only the short-term interests of the rich.

In recent years, Jeremy Seabrook (1985) has written much to raise our awareness of the role of consumerism in buying our consent to the economic and political *status quo*. He describes how it manufactures and diffuses a kind of ignorance which, as we have seen, conceals the real nature of the products we buy. A look around any town centre shopping arcade on a Saturday afternoon, suggests that young people are particularly susceptible to the culture of consumerism. Yet this is profoundly anti-educational; appealing to wants rather than needs, offering only temporary satisfactions and suppressing knowledge which could inform real choice. At the same time, consumerism generates a new kind of poverty for those who are unable to participate. It has eroded the old socialist values of mutual aid and community and left many people lonely and uncared for in our midst. The definition of need has passed to capital and as the majority become willing workers and consumers on its accelerating treadmill of production and consumption, real needs go unmet. The costs of consumerism fall on the poor in our inner cities and villages just as they do on the workers in the South who labour for low reward to provide the raw materials and products our consumerism demands. Making young people aware of these costs should surely form a significant part of any programme of social education.

What We Consume

In 1984, I was asked to coordinate part of the World Wildlife Fund-UK's Global Environmental Education Programme. A module *What We Consume* would provide ten curriculum units for 11-16 year old pupils each linking a product we consume to an issue of environment and development in another part of the world. By a suitable choice of products or commodity chains, it was hoped the module could sample the major themes of the 'World and UK Conservation Strategies' and introduce pupils to the social use of nature within the main forms of political economy found around the world. For example, a tin of corned beef would link pupils to the destruction of rainforest in Brazil and the development priorities of a military regime in a country undergoing dependent development on the semi-periphery of the world economy. Buying a Band Aid record would link them to Ethiopia, desertification and the policies of a centralist Marxist government in a country being actively under-developed on the periphery of Soviet imperialism. While seven of the units would focus on environment and development in nation states, there would also be an introductory unit, *Society and Nature*, and two concluding units which would deal with attempts to ameliorate environmental problems by multi-lateral action from above, and attempts to create ecologically sustainable development by grassroots action from below.

The Curriculum framework

What We Consume has been much influenced by Ira Shor's ideas on critical teaching and everyday life (Shor, 1980). He suggests that teachers should encourage pupils to reflect on ordinary, everyday situations so that they 're-experience the ordinary' or become aware of their true social significance. In the case of the beefburger already examined, this would mean becoming aware of the location of junk food within a network of economic and social relations which carry high costs for many. Awareness should lead to reconstruction; Shor would encourage pupils to redesign convenience food, render it socially and ecologically acceptable, and carry their proposals forward by making new demands from the school canteen for example. Shor's method stresses structural thinking or the ability to locate everyday situations and things within a network of economic and political relations. If teachers and pupils are to develop such thinking they will find it necessary to ask appropriate questions and develop certain concepts.

To encourage structural thinking, *What We Consume* makes use of the curriculum framework of key questions and concepts set out in Figure 1. This was derived from an understanding of the world order and issues of environment and development, set out in the teachers' handbook, and from ideas developed by Adrian Leftwich (1983) in his book *Redefining Politics*. The questions focus attention on the social use of nature within different systems of economic production, distribution and redistribution, power and decision making, social organization, and culture and ideology. They encourage teachers and pupils to regard the environment as being socially constructed, to recognize that the environmental costs of production and development are unevenly shared, and to realize that a transition to ecologically sustainable development requires fundamental economic, political, and cultural change if it is not to sustain or increase inequalities. The link between ecodevelopment and the extension of the economic and political democracy is a theme which runs through all the units of *What We Consume*. Readers may find it useful to spend a few minutes applying the questions and concepts in Figure 1 to an environment and development issue with which they are familiar.

Key ideas
Teachers and pupils use *What We Consume*'s key questions and concepts while examining the *key ideas* which form the core of each unit. Figure 2 lists the key ideas from unit five which deals with the cattle frontier in Brazil's north west. In each unit a curriculum matrix shows how its ten classroom activities are designed to sample key questions and ideas.

Political literacy
In carrying out *What We Consume*'s activities, pupils will clearly develop knowledge, skills, and attitudes which contribute to

political literacy. The *Programme for Political Education* (Porter, 1983) was another major influence on the project and Figure 3 is an attempt to show how the units fit that programme's framework. Readers not familiar with the diagram on which Figure 3 is based will find the original in many of the Programme's publications.

Classroom activities

A curriculum designed to promote structural thinking and economic and political democracy, must clearly encourage democratic classrooms. World Studies has probably done most in recent years to encourage experiential learning in development education, and *What We Consume* has drawn heavily on its philosophy and repertoire of teaching activities. Five examples of activities, drawn from a number of the project's units, illustrate the approach:

ET's View of the World Pupils imagine they are an extra-terrestrial approaching planet earth. They can call up information about the planet on an onboard computer. What can they deduce about life and environment on planet earth? The activity introduces basic facts about the global economy, environment issues, and inequalities in the world.

Introducing Environmental Politics Pupils are given role cards and represent three imaginary political parties; Enterprise, Citizen, and Fair Deal. They have to formulate policies on environmental issues and compare them with the policies of real political parties. This activity gives an introduction to political ideologies and the different meanings of environmental values.

An Adventure Game Small groups of pupils represent a migrant family in Brazil. Using an adventure game format they have to make decisions about moving to Rondonia and what to do when they get there. They learn of the desperate choices facing such a family.

Education or Indoctrination? A story from a Chinese picture book for children has been cut up into individual pictures. Pupils must now arrange these in the right order to tell a story. The story carries a message about the need to care collectively for the environment.

Sorting Out Opinions Pupils match statements about development in Amazonia to a list of characters whose backgrounds are described. In doing so they learn of the different interest groups present in Brazil.

Changing the curriculum

There have been few attempts to implement the ideas provided by radical theorists in curriculum studies and environment and development. The teachers involved with *What We Consume* have tended to resist structural thinking, have too readily dismissed it as too difficult for their pupils, and have dwelt on what is safe and descriptive rather than that which is controversial and theoretical. Nevertheless we have taught each other a good deal and it is hoped that the book *What We Consume* (Huckle, 1987) will make some of this experience available for others.

The transition to socialism requires the rebuilding of a popular socialist movement and the reconstruction of a socialist culture. There are signs of the latter in some elements of youth culture, for example in lyrics of the pop group, The Housemartins. All is not lost and clearly schooling has a role to play in cultural criticism and reconstruction. *What We Consume* is designed to play a part in this. It can counter the all pervasive messages of consumerism, expose the real costs of the way we live, and suggest more just and democratic alternatives. In a small way, it is a response to the issues which this book considers. In the present debate over the core curriculum, our task is to convince a growing number of parents, communities, politicians and others, that such a curriculum is necessary for all young people. It can help them to understand and act on the major issues of environment and development facing the world and is arguably more relevant and socially useful than much that will find a ready place within the core. While many would suggest that advocates of socially critical education are currently in retreat, it remains a vital part of the struggle for a more democratic, just and ecologically sustainable future.

Figure 1: The Project's Key Questions and Concepts

A Economic Production
  A1. What natural resources are being used or conserved?
  A2. For what purposes are they being used or conserved? By whom, how, and why?
  A3. What is the impact of economic production on the environment? What environments does it produce?
  A4. Is the production ecologically sustainable?
  A5. Is the production socially useful? Does it meet people's basic needs?
  A6. Who owns and controls the natural resources and technology used in economic production?
  A7. What power do workers have to decide what is made and how it is produced?
  A8. In what ways is economic production changing and how is this likely to affect the use of nature in the future?
  A9. How does the society's history and present position within the world economy, shape its production, development, and use of nature?
Sample concepts: nature, ecosystem, land, land use, natural resource, renewable

resource, non-renewable resource, resource conservation, labour, energy, capital, technology, alternative technology, ecologically sustainable production, economic development, industrialization, needs, wants, ownership, economic power, economic democracy, division of labour, capitalism, profit, market, socialism, economic planning, state collectivism, world economy, interdependence, commodity chains, multinational company, colonialism, imperialism, unequal exchange, global division of labour, dependent development, economic recession, product cycle.

B Distribution and Redistribution

B1. How are the benefits and costs of economic production distributed and redistributed? What principles determine this and what methods are used to bring it about?

B2. What is the level of inequality in society? Are differences in wealth and environmental well being increasing or decreasing?

B3. Is poverty a cause of environmental damage?

B4. Does wealth result in wasteful production and environmental damage?

B5. What amount of wealth is used for environmental research, management, and conservation? How is the charge for this distributed?

B6. Would redistribution of wealth and greater equality within society assist a transition to ecologically sustainable production and development?

B7. How is the society involved in transfers of trade, investment, technology, loans, and aid?

B8. Do these transfers help or hinder the society in moving towards ecologically sustainable production and development?

B9. Would a redistribution of wealth and greater equality between societies, assist moves towards ecodevelopment?

Sample concepts: wealth, waste, poverty, environmental poverty, equality/inequality, scarcity/surplus, supply, demand, population, consumption, conservation, trade, investment, aid, social welfare, justice, environmental management, international economic order, competition/co-operation, arms, arms trade.

C Power and Decision Making

C1. How is the society governed?

C2. How does government regulate the use of nature?

C3. How does government plan and manage the environment? What institutions and procedures exist for this? How are decisions made? How are conflicts over the environment resolved or managed?

C4. What power do people have to participate in political decision making? How is political power distributed in society and according to what procedures and rules is it used?

C5. In what ways does environmental politics reflect the power and interests of different groups in society? What policies and strategies do environmental groups adopt in seeking to influence the political process?

C6. What forms of economic development does the government support? In what way are the government's economic and foreign policies related to the society's role in the world economy?

C7. In what ways do the government's economic, foreign, and other policies shape its policies on the environment?

C8. In what ways does the international political system seek to resolve global environmental problems? Does competition between nation states prevent international action on environmental problems?

C9. In what ways do environmentalists seek to influence the international political system?

Sample concepts: politics, power/powerlessness, nation state, local state, international politics, government, forms of government, parties, pressure groups, law, force, authority, manipulation, reason, co-operation/conflict, representation, democracy, consultation, corruption, participation, bureaucracy.

D Social Organization

D1. What distinct groups exist in society and what amounts of economic and political power do they have at their disposal? Which groups suffer from a lack of power?

D2. Are there movements working to extend democracy; to give more people some control of economic production and political decision making?

D3. What form do these movements take? What are their aims and tactics?

D4. Do the movements incorporate environmental goals? What issues do they tackle? How effective are they?

D5. What groups work with environmentalists in such movements? What part do women play? What part do ethnic minorities play?

D6. Which groups in society oppose such movements for greater democracy and what actions do they take?

D7. What have the movements learnt from their campaigns?

D8. Do the movements co-operate at all levels, including the international level?

Sample concepts: individual, family, community, class, racism, patriarchy, social order/disorder, consent/dissent, social control, social movements, environmental movement, voluntary groups, trade union, consumer organizations, social responsibility, appropriate technology, co-option.

E Culture and Ideology

E1. What are the accepted ways of interacting with, and thinking about, nature and the environment?

E2. In what ways is the society's culture and ideology being changed by economic development? What role do external forces play in this?

E3. How does technology reflect and shape people's relations with nature? What alternative or appropriate technology would alter these relations?

E4. How do ideas from the natural and social sciences, and from other areas of knowledge, reflect and shape our relations with nature? What ideas are taught in schools? What ideas are not taught? Which ideas act as ideology?

E5. What ideas are used by groups and parties engaged in environmental politics? How do these ideas reflect material interests?

E6. What messages about nature, the environment, and the world, does popular culture transmit? What role does popular culture play in consumerism and imperialism?

E7. To what extent do news media explain the real causes of problems relating to development and the environment?

E8. What elements of traditional, minority, and alternative cultures could be useful in creating an ecologically sustainable society?

Sample concepts: cultural needs, communication, language, custom, tradition, religion, myth, values, moral code, world view, knowledge, science, social science, advertising, popular culture, consumer culture, political culture, education, environmental education, culture contact, cultural imperialism.

Figure 2: Key Ideas – Unit 5 Brazil

1. Between 1964 and 1984, Brazil's military government pursued a policy of rapid economic development aided by trans-national corporations. It provided subsidies for domestic and foreign capital to 'open up' Amazonia. This policy reduced pressure for land reform in north-east and south Brazil, sustained Brazilian nationalism, and sought to reduce Brazil's mounting international debt problems.

2. Large areas of Amazonia are currently frontier territory where conflict between forest indians, old and new settlers, and powerful agricultural and mining interests, leads to open conflict. Both indians and forest are disappearing at an alarming rate.

3. The clearance of tropical moist forest, and its replacement by ranching, leads to complex environmental change. Ranching brings short term benefits, is not ecologically sustainable, and has a productivity and employment potential much lower than the forest.

4. The indian protection agency, FUNAI, has proved relatively powerless compared with the land development agency, INCRA. Pressure from such international agencies as the World Bank have brought about some change, and the indians themselves are becoming increasingly militant.

5. The ecological/environmental protection functions and genetic wealth of tropical moist forest are of great economic value. Indigenous forest dwellers know how to derive a sustained living from their environment, and their knowledge should inform ecologically sustainable development.

6. The commitment of Brazil's new government to land reform and an extension of democracy is not yet clear. Rubber tappers' demands for sustainable forest use do provide the government with an early opportunity to rethink its policy concerning Amazonian development.

Attitudes and Procedural Values	Skills	Knowledge	

Attitudes and Procedural Values

1. Willingness to be critical of estimates of the deforested area in Amazonia (5).
2. Willingness to give reasons why one agrees, or disagrees, with the policies of the Tigray Liberation Front (6), or uses private rather than public transport (5).
3. Respect for evidence that the Soviet Union has attempted to clean up Lake Baikal (8).
4. Willingness to change one's attitudes and values when confronted with new evidence on the causes of famine in Ethiopia. (6).
5. Value fairness when reaching a decision on whether or not to buy goods from a firm which imports hard woods from Brazil (5).
6. Value the freedom of trade unionists to influence the nature of work and economic production (10).
7. Tolerate a diversity of ideas, beliefs, values and interests about possible futures for the UK countryside (4).

Skills

Intellectual skills

1. Ability to interpret and evaluate information and evidence from different sources on acid rain (9).
2. Ability to use political concepts & ideas to organize information about the Countryside Commission (4).
3. Ability to apply reasoning skills to the problems of food surpluses & construct sound arguments for restructuring the CAP (4).
4. Ability to perceive the consequences of taking or not taking, direct action in order to prevent the felling of forests (10).

Action skills

1. Ability to participate in a group decision concerning migration in Brazil (5).
2. Ability to use local government in order to create a 'greener' town (8).

Communication skills

1. Ability to design a newspaper page supporting or opposing Government policy on acid rain (9).
2. Ability to participate in a discussion on the real value of Band Aid (6).
3. Ability to perceive and understand the interests, beliefs and views of environmentalists supporting different political parties (1).
4. Ability to exercise empathy with a school pupil in China (8) a shopper in Moscow (7) or a family in Brazil (5).

Knowledge

Professional knowledge

1. The structure of power within the UN system as it affects the review of the Antarctic Treaty (9).
2. How disputes over access to farmers' land are settled in the UK (4).
3. How disputes over economic policy & development are settled in China (8).
4. Where the resources of UNEP come from and how they are used (9).
5. The possible consequences should dockland communities in London be given resources to plan and develop their own environment (10).
6. How some local government authorities in Britain have spent more on the environment and job creation than that the national Government considers necessary (10).
7. How some rubber tappers in Brazil have promoted sustainable development policies for forest areas (5).

Practical knowledge and understanding

1. The differing values, goals & methods of the CEGB, UK Government and Greenpeace, in the dispute over acid rain (9).
2. The possible danger of pesticide residues on our food & the failure of politicians to impose and enforce adequate controls (1).
3. How poverty and desertification in Ethiopia is linked to the foreign policies of other nations, including those of the USSR (6).
4. How to lobby one's MEP in an attempt to influence the restructuring of the CAP. Knowledge of how to use the local press to draw public attention to one's views (4).
5. A developing understanding of the decision-making process in a state collectivist economy, and the meaning of democracy within such societies (6, 7, 8).
6. Knowledge of how to obtain information about environmental pressure groups and their policies (several units).

Note: *Numbers in brackets refer to the units in* What We Consume.

References

Huckle, J. (1987) *What We Consume*. Richmond Publishing/World Wildlife Fund-UK.

Leftwich, A. (1983) *Redefining Politics*. Methuen.

Porter, A. (1983) *Principles of Political Literacy; the Working Papers of the Programme for Political Education*. London University Institute of Education.

Seabrook, J. (1985) Fast Food, Junk Morality. In *New Socialist* March.

Shor, I. (1980) *Critical Teaching and Everyday Life*. South End Press.

CONCLUSION
The Case for an Education Network

Colin Lacey and Roy Williams

> The radical change in human attitudes foreseen by the acceptance of the concept of sustainable development depends on a vast campaign of public education and re-education, a worldwide debate around these vital life and death issues.
>
> Gro Harlem Brundtland
> The World Commission on Environment and Development

The conclusions and proposals emerging from the contributions to this volume are summarized in this first section of the conclusion. They range, in part one, from Michael Redclift's desire for an 'alternative project' which redefines the managerial solution to problems of development and environment by giving new powers and responsibilities to indigenous populations (the new solutions would draw on traditional cultures rather than destroying them) to David Pepper's radical environmental curriculum. In the second part they range from Colin Lacey's desire to see a socialist curriculum take its proper place in schools alongside the present capitalist curriculum to Andy Hargreaves' practical advice on assessment and Geoff Whitty's description of how to persevere and prevail in your negotiations with an examination board. The field is truly immense and it would seem almost impossible to suggest a simple set of outcomes that could promote such a wide variety of suggestions. Yet this is what our seminar succeeded in doing.

The papers contained in this book form a set of responses to some of the issues to be found in the examination of the relationship between environment, development and public education. They not only reflect the personal experience and understanding of the contributors but, taken as a whole, provide a collective resonance with the notion expressed in the above quotation. The systems and processes of education are failing to engender the necessary radical changes required because they are not part of the debate and are reluctant to embark upon a programme of self-education which would lead to their effective renewal as a force for that change.

We learned from the introduction and from the chapters in the first part of the book that the global political economy, with its attendant ideologies and forms of production and consumption, practises a form of dynamic conservatism as a means to maintain the hegemony of a minority over a majority in the use of power and the exploitation of resources worldwide. Progressive, sustainable development, interpreted within the context of the present geopolitical arrangement of economic, political and cultural systems, has meaning only for those who possess the power and the wealth to impose their particular versions of such development. The resulting contradictions are manifestly evident and support the concerns and arguments which are expressed in the papers written by Lacey, Redclift and Abraham. Their views and analyses provide the substance of an argument for a new agenda for education and this is further reinforced by the critical assessment of environmental education put forward in Pepper's chapter. If present educational systems, with their present policies and practices, are not to continue to replicate the dominant ethos of one system of control over all others, then the need for a re-evaluation of the human/environment relationship is an imperative in the design and development of a curriculum commensurate with a new environmentalism.

In addition to the contradictions which are created by the imbalances that exist within the global system, there are specific tensions which derive from the interaction of the structures and forces that manipulate elements in the system. Knowledge and understanding of these is a key feature in the programme of re-education for attitudinal change required by the espousal of the concept of sustainable development. The beginning of a necessary intervention from the formation and adoption of new and alternative perspectives, through a major shift in the structures, purposes and practices of educational systems, is a step that must be taken. This was advocated by all the contributors to part one and provides the theme for consideration by the writers in part two. In this part of the book educationalists had their say, exploring the issues of teaching and learning about environment and development from their particular perspectives within the education system.

The papers presented are concerned with both theory and practice and the influence of ideology and procedures for control over the arrangements for schooling. The deep-seated and pervasive constraints and obstructions which work against any attempt for radical reform are identified and examined in the papers from Lacey and Hargreaves, whereas those of Huckle and Whitty present accounts of approaches employed in a more practical context. All of the papers recognize that the pursuit of the reform and reconstruction of educational systems as a prerequisite for an engagement with environment and development problems on a world scale is a political activity. Education and schooling, with its adjuncts of learning and teaching, create and sustain value systems that foster the attitudes which govern our relationships to the world in which we live. An education imprisoned within the consciousness of a world view and which utilizes its instruments of control to support and perpetuate intellectual, ethical and societal frameworks in the unquestioning maintenance of that view, abdicates its true responsibility.

There are a number of propositions to be gleaned from the contributions to this volume concerning the needs expressed in the quotation that introduced this section. There is no dissent from the notion that attitudes have to be changed, or that the concept of sustainable development is integral to the debate on the survival of the planet, or that one of the means for achieving one and promoting the other is through a system of education. For all the contributors, the deficiencies of the education process, both in substance and pedagogy, in addressing the human-ecology-development problem, result from its function as a preserver of the *status quo*, especially where the issues and problems that seek curriculum space have political and ethical dimensions. Perhaps, more significantly, for those who practise education across the whole of its spectrum are those acts of enclosure and foreclosure that those in power implement to stifle debate and forestall re-education. In recognition of this closing-off of areas of vital concern, whether deliberately or inadvertently, the proposition that some measure of 'glasnost' should be injected into institutions and practices of education, as a necessary condition for its renewal and reconstruction, should have no opposition. For the world and all that inhabit it, now and in the future, the doors that are bolted and barred to alternative and different ideas need to be opened. Ideas about how the world should be ordered and conducted; about what constitutes valid knowledge and appropriate values; about what innovative and creative ideas should penetrate the curriculum offerings, not only of schools and other formal education institutions, but of all the other structures in society that bend, and mould, and shape, and control the ways in which people think and behave towards each other and towards the world in which they live.

During our discussions with the contributors to this book it became clear that we were studying the interrelations of social and natural systems and hoping to influence one of them (the education system) so that changes within it would influence the others (development and the environment). Yet when we focused our attention on influencing the education system (the first step on the journey) the immensity of the task rendered any one or even any group of our suggestions inadequate. As we turned our attention to the peculiar qualities of social systems and their resistance to change the nature of our predicament became clear. Social systems are complex interconnected sets of relationships. The relationships are constrained by rules, expectations and habitual behaviour. Any one person within such a system is held in place by a multitude of connections and expectations. Even hardworking, talented teachers find it difficult, within modern institutions like schools, to clear enough space for changing small elements of their own behaviour. It requires considerable energy and resources to coordinate these changes with others who might not wish to change or have other ideas about the direction in which change is required. It is often the case, for example, that teachers find it impossible to get to the first base, that is, to find a small group of likeminded people who can agree on the direction of change. However, once this is achieved there are still many other stages to negotiate before a successful innovation is born. Social systems are held in place by multiple constraints acting from within and from without.

It became clear that to initiate change or even create a climate in which change could be more fruitfully discussed it would be necessary to set up an organization that had many of the same characteristics of a social system. It would need to impinge on the education system at a number of different levels, simultaneously. It would also need to influence the context in which the social system existed and create an intellectual climate in which the proposed change was sympathetically understood. It became clear that the kind of organization we were discussing would need to be more complex and pervasive than a curriculum development project; it would need to unite sympathizers who work in a number of institutions and professions both inside and outside of the education system. We were, in fact, talking about an education network which could unite sympathetic teachers and people from other professions and which could articulate with other organizations. As we clarified its structure and purpose a number of salient features became clear.

1. It would require a broad unifying philosophy capable of bringing together educators and people with varied interests and differing political views. It should be capable of accommodating the interests of socialists, radicals, and

reformists interested in a wide variety of topics from development and ecology to human rights and alternative medicine, insofar as they were seen to be relevant to education.

2. It would need to draw on the research and experience of people working in a wide range of institutions from higher education, schools and research institutes through interest and pressure groups, voluntary agencies and charities to public and private institutions involved in broadcasting, publishing and industry.

3. It would need to develop processes through which a debate could establish common aims and purposes and make them available for people who wished to join.

4. The process of information exchange and mutual support could be developed to support its membership in a wide variety of ways. For example, the teacher looking for authoritative sources and relevant material for the classroom; the research biologist looking for ways of making his or her research more accessible to school children; the television producer looking for an informed group of teachers and audience feedback; the publisher looking for an author and even the politician looking for reliable judgements and up-to-date research.

5. Within these general activities the network should sponsor events such as: seminars, major and minor publications, television programmes and school based curriculum development. It should publish a newsletter.

In order to start constructing an association with such a wide spread of membership yet with an aim focused on reform of the curriculum and the organization of schools, it was clearly necessary to think about starting from a particular area of concern. The areas chosen coincided with the focus of the seminar (which led to the publication of this book) on ecology and development – but with the intention of developing into other areas as soon as the resources and opportunity arose.

The seminar endorsed the need to develop a theoretical or speculative basis on which the network could be established. The seven papers in this book therefore constitute the beginning of a debate in which a large number of issues will be brought forward so that their relevance to the education of young people can be demonstrated. For example, the notion of an inner ecology so well developed by John Abraham in Chapter 1.2, establishes quite clearly the importance of terms like food additives and prepared foods as an issue of concern for young people. In addition, he points to the similarities between the effects of highly developed prepacked manufactured foods and the developing business of agrochemicals and plant packages which also add chemicals to our diet via the residues of fertilizer and pesticide which are increasingly seen as a necessary ingredient of 'advanced' agriculture. These issues relate closely to the curriculum development described by John Huckle in 'What we consume'. In these two papers we therefore have the beginning of a curriculum objective – to establish and explore the concept of 'inner ecology' and relate it to major developments in economic and ecological systems.

This illustration is, of course, speculative and anticipatory, but it demonstrates how new exciting ideas can arise from the kind of cross fertilization produced in a seminar and how this would be multiplied within the framework of an education network. The process of development by the network can be taken forward a few more speculative steps.

The identification of an organizing concept like 'inner ecology' would stimulate the network in two directions. The first would be to bring together people researching in the fields of nutrition, food additives and diet with people working in the area of agriculture, agrieconomics and development. Seminars and the resulting papers would provide the materials for the second step. Teachers and educationalists would be asked to develop classroom materials from the outcomes of the seminars and to pose new questions to, and make new demands on, the researchers. In this way teachers and their pupils would be linked to the research frontiers of appropriate disciplines. Their role would be to convey their current concerns and take a critical approach to the results of research. The gain for researchers would be a break-down of the isolation of research and a development in skills of communication to interested outsiders. The increase in rewards and excitement could be substantial for all concerned.

If a development of this kind grew and bore fruit, a second level of connections and influence would occur within a network established along the lines described earlier. Connections could be made to people working in the media who would both describe (report) and enhance the development process. If these events harnessed and sustained public interest a further stage could involve politicians and new policy development. Finally a highly speculative, long-term development could involve changes in food manufacturing regulations, forms of social control over the production of food and cultural challenge to manufactured foods. The various stages of this network development are illustrated in Figure 1.

While the description of this development is unashamed speculation and extrapolation, it does provide a model for the future and more importantly gives us an understanding of the kinds of agreements and principles on which the network should be based. It is important to return to the more immediate task – the establishment of the 'broad unifying philosophy', capable of bringing together people with a wide variety of radical and reforming aims. A lot of guidance can be obtained from the papers in this book and the concerns raised in the introduction are also of great importance in leading us towards 'the broad unifying philosophy'.

Figure 1: Stages in the Network Development

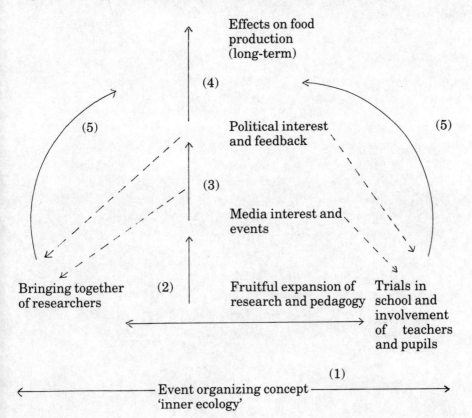